Eyes Pried Open:

Rookie FBI Agent

Former Special Agent:

Vincent Sellers

BLACK ROSE
writing™

ISBN: 978-1-61296-440-9

PUBLISHED BY BLACK ROSE WRITING

www.blackrosewriting.com

Printed in the United States of America

Suggested retail price $16.95

Eyes Pried Open: Rookie FBI Agent is printed in Book Antiqua

This book is dedicated to the analysts, staff, and agents of the FBI who live their lives with Fidelity, Bravery, and Integrity for benefit of the citizens of the United States of America.

Special thanks to my "bro," Ken;

my parents, Kenneth and Martha;

and my true partner in crime, Jennifer.

Eyes Pried Open:

Rookie FBI Agent

CHAPTERS

Part I: Becoming an FBI Agent and the FBI Academy

Part II: Adjusting to Life as a New Agent

Part III: Never a Dull Moment

Part IV: The End of the FBI Dream

Part V: Epilogue

Introduction

I love the FBI. I love the people who make up the FBI. I believe in the mission of the FBI. But this book is not a love note to the FBI. Instead, my intent is to provide a normal person's perspective of being a Special Agent in the FBI. Many seasoned agents have written excellent books singing high praises for the Bureau. Other agents have happily shared their negative views of the FBI. My intent is simply to provide an honest account of my time in the Bureau and of how that journey impacted me. In a sense, my eyes were "pried open" as I was exposed to the inner workings of the FBI and the underbelly of society, working as an agent on a violent crimes squad. You will not be reading embellished tales of heroism. I never shot anybody, nor did anybody shoot at me. I did not rappel out of helicopters. I did not work alongside Special Agent Starling, nor did I interrogate Hannibal Lecter. I never crossed paths with Special Agents Scully or Mulder, nor did I come across any X-Files. I never deactivated a terrorist bomb at the last possible second. But I did have some fun, and did learn about crime, about our country, and about myself. I was just a normal corporate guy who successfully pursued a childhood dream, and this is my story. I hope you will enjoy it.

Vincent Sellers
Austin, Texas
August, 2014

Part I

Becoming an FBI Agent and the FBI Academy

CHAPTER 1

The Dream

Snow covered the wooded hillsides. A peaceful winter wonderland enveloped my Chevy pickup as I cruised through the Virginia countryside, yet I was more nervous and scared than I had ever been in my life. But my extreme apprehension was topped by sheer excitement that one experiences only a few times in life. I took the exit marked "Quantico," and began the chapter in my life that I had dreamed about, but had never believed could come true.

To get to this point, I had spent a full year focused on making it into the FBI. It had been one year almost to the day since I had submitted my application to become an FBI agent. I was thrilled to have been invited to Phase 1 testing, the first of three phases required to become an agent. I showed up at the Alamodome in San Antonio, Texas, and was met with a long line of at least one hundred candidates. Out of this crowd, which was already funneled down from a large applicant pool to a select group of qualified candidates, only a few would be invited for the next phase of testing.

I chose to sit at the very front of the massive testing room, which was roughly the size of a high school gymnasium. I sat right in front of the agents who administered the test. I paid close attention. I did not ask any dumb questions. I was polite and truly thankful merely to be there with the opportunity to become an agent, no matter how slim the odds of success were. I took the Phase 1 exam with determination and worked every second allowed to answer the multiple choice questions correctly. Most of the questions fell into categories of math, logic, and personality. There were far too many questions to finish in time, but like everyone else, I gave it my absolute all.

I was not aware at the time, but I would later learn that for the next phase of the application process, candidates would submit a photo along with additional in-depth application content. Although I will never know if my front-of-the-room seating choice provided any advantage in being selected for Phase 2, the required photo could potentially identify candidates who made an impression, either positive or negative, during the first round of testing. That next phase was the most critical, because if selected, the candidates would be given the green light by the FBI to become agents. They still had plenty of hurdles to clear, in the form of a written test, verbal test, physical test, medical test, and background check. But the odds of becoming an agent suddenly jumped to about one in four, versus the roughly one in five-hundred odds with which the applicant started the application process. The person's destiny would finally be in his or her own hands, rather than depending on getting lucky or getting his or her resume noticed out of a giant stack of competitors' entries.

The toughest part about applying is the waiting. The FBI, unlike most other jobs, is the dream of those who apply: seemingly a lifetime of happiness doing something worthwhile versus the drudgery of most professions that are endured simply, as my mother used to say, "to make a living." As a corporate warrior, with years of experience shuffling among a never-ending maze of cubes that had started to feel like jail cells, I felt drawn to do something special and amazing. Software implementation projects, financial analysis, and improving business processes for ten years were mind-numbing. I had recently endured a breakup in my marriage, along with the death of my father. I was at a moment in my life where I was ready to make a dramatic transition to a more fulfilling career. At the time, I felt that if I did not make it into the FBI, my life would be incomplete, and it was hard to imagine being truly satisfied with my life if I were forced to remain in the confines of the white-collar worker's world.

So after what felt like an eternity but was really only three weeks, I received notification that I had passed the Phase 1 exam. I was instructed to fill out and return a more detailed application along with a photo. I immediately went to work.

I knew that a very well-prepared application, along with an attention-grabbing resume, would increase my odds of being noticed and invited to participate in a Phase 2 interview. I worked an entire weekend on my application, and sent it to my local FBI office in San Antonio via USPS Priority Mail. I beat the deadline by a couple of weeks, and knew that my application was one of the first (possibly the very first) received out of the Phase 1 group who had passed. By my estimate, taking into consideration the large number of applicants, if there were a stack of fifty applications, I figured my odds were roughly one in ten of getting picked.

In the meantime, while feeling pleased about my perceived progression down the hiring funnel, I decided to end any questions whether my uncorrected vision was at least the 20/200 required by the FBI. My eyesight was 20/300, and did not meet the vision standard. I did not want to make it through one of the most rigorous application processes in the world, only to be turned away because of a literal lack of vision. So I signed up for a LASIK procedure and within a week was getting my vision corrected. I had a rough go at that appointment, with the doctor saying I was only the second person out of 28,000 who had eye sockets that were not compatible with the LASIK equipment. However, the doctor was able to "freehand" (in his own words) and complete the procedure. Afterwards, my vision was not 20/20 uncorrected but was good enough to pass the FBI vision test with flying colors. I was initially disturbed to be one of the only unlucky people ever to experience the LASIK issues. However, when I realized that I did walk away with much better vision, I chalked the experience up to being a good omen;

perhaps I would be one of the relatively few lucky souls to make it into the FBI.

Two months later I got the call that I was picked for Phase 2 examination. I knew that I interviewed and tested well, and for the first time I thought my odds were better than 50/50 of becoming an agent. My dream was coming true. Nothing could have made my steps become lighter than knowing that I had an excellent chance of being an FBI agent. This feeling of joy trumped the personal sadness that I had been dealing with. I knew I was heading for better things, both professionally and personally.

Around this time, I began to seriously consider the physical testing involved in becoming an agent. I was an excellent runner, although I was slightly overweight and out of shape. I had never excelled at the other exercises that I would be tested on: namely, pushups, sit-ups, and pull-ups. The time had come to get into shape.

I began a regimen of running eight miles every other day, with pushups and sit-ups on my non-running days. Over the next few months, my weight dropped, my strength improved, and I felt better mentally and physically than I ever had in my life. I could almost feel myself morphing into an FBI agent.

My local FBI field office met with several candidates, including me, who were scheduled for the Phase 2 test. The office recommended a plan to think of answers to questions that were likely to be asked and suggested we prepare written and oral statements to gear up for the test. I wrote page after page of examples of life challenges, work problems, leadership scenarios, and other typical corporate human-resource-style questions that I anticipated potentially being questioned about. I followed the recommended "who what when why how" method, and prepared by giving oral statements while video recording myself. I would go back and listen to my answers and evaluate my body language, and through this iterative process I prepared for the biggest interview of my life.

Meanwhile, I continued to walk the corridors of cube-world.

Although I was extremely fond of my coworkers, and despite working for a highly respected and well-run organization, I was disenchanted with the corporate culture, which is captured accurately and humorously by movies like *Office Space* and cartoons like *Dilbert*. A few of my company's policies and rules were ludicrous: *Dilbert* cartoons were banned from being put on cube walls. Another policy specified a maximum of two photographs per cube, with size limitations. I could feel myself longing for more meaningful and satisfying employment by the day. And I knew that if I didn't make it into the FBI, it would be the greatest disappointment of my life.

The time finally arrived for the Phase 2 test. Several other applicants and I flew to Kansas City, Missouri, for the test. We were a small group but immediately found commonality and camaraderie. We knew that some of us would be appointed as FBI agents, and others would be left with nothing but tales of "how I almost became an FBI agent."

My level of nervousness on the morning of the exam was at record levels. The only comparable anxiety-ridden times I had ever experienced were the instant the gate was about the drop while racing motocross, and the split-second when you are climbing to an open door of an airplane in flight before skydiving. Terrifying, yes, but I also felt an adrenaline rush. I remember walking down the corridor of the hotel, dressed like an FBI agent, and I felt myself becoming an agent. I even had a crowd cheering. And in my heart, everyone who had played a part in my life was with me, especially my father who had died two years previously. Using a black marker, I wrote the names of friends and family on my body, in a strange and superstitious pre-game ritual. To put it mildly, I wanted desperately to be an FBI agent. I was summoning spirits that I did not even believe in. Nothing was going to stop me.

I was "on" that day. I first took the written exam, which went extremely well. I cannot divulge the contents of the exam, but I can say it was unlike any test I had ever taken before. This critical test was an essay exam, the type of test with which I was most comfortable. The test-taker had to not merely write, but also use logic. Seeing the various layers of complexity within the exam, I surmised that if someone made it to the higher "levels," that enhanced the applicant's score. I could tell that I made it to every level, exactly as time expired. I had aced the written test, but the toughest part remained.

The oral exam was an hour long interview in front of a panel of three FBI agents. At this point, I had only met a few agents in my life; I was in awe of them. They also scared me. The interview began. I sat in front of a tape recorder, which almost seemed more like a Hollywood-borrowed FBI intimidation scare tactic than a functional part of the interview. At least there was not a bright overhead spotlight focused on me, which was the movie cliché that I almost expected. I was asked roughly fifteen questions, most of which were questions that I had anticipated. I gracefully danced through some questions and stumbled through others. I took advantage of the rules of the interview which allowed the test taker to skip questions. This strategy seemed like a great idea until I was down to the last ten minutes of the interview, with the last three remaining questions being ones that I had bypassed because I did not have an answer for them. I had fifty strong minutes with a lousy ten minute finale. I hoped that I would be judged more on my initial responses than on my final impression.

I was relieved to have completed the Phase 2 exam process. I flew back to Texas, obsessing over every detail of the testing process, replaying questions and the answers I had provided. The more time that passed, the more I figured that I had failed miserably. Time seemed to come to a complete stand-still for the next week. I was so anxious to receive word from the FBI that I even took my cell phone with me when I went running, which certainly was not my normal practice.

One day I was running in a greenbelt behind my housing subdivision, when the phone rang, showing me that the FBI was calling. I felt like my life had come down to this moment.

"Is Vince there?"

"Yes, that's me!" I gasped since I had just run a two mile time trial, in the hot August Texas afternoon heat.

"You passed Phase 2. Congratulations!"

I didn't even know what to say, or how I should feel, but I knew that those words meant that I was *conditionally* appointed as a Special Agent of the FBI. "Happy" does not begin to describe my emotions. In my head, I did a faithful Leo DeCaprio (from *Titanic*) impression --- at that moment I was "THE KING OF THE WORLD!"

CHAPTER 2

The Polygraph

"Who are you, the Pope?"

I had never been asked this question before. Definitely not by an intimidating FBI agent, who was grilling me while I was strapped in a chair resembling a death-row electric chair. This seemed to be a scene right out of the show *24*, and unfortunately I was not remotely armed with Jack Bauer's confidence or skills.

Yes, I had made it to the infamous polygraph exam portion of becoming an FBI agent. After leading a life that would have made me almost eligible for sainthood, I could not imagine having anything to worry about. I was told that the best way to prepare for the polygraph was NOT to prepare. In other words, the less an applicant thought and obsessed about the test, the less likely he or she was to be stressed by the questions; theoretically the candidate should theoretically pass the test with ease. But this theory proved not to be fact, at least for me.

Earlier that morning, a couple of weeks after passing the Phase 2 examination, I had met with other candidates, and we were put through our paces and tested on running, pushups, sit-ups, and pull-ups. I enjoyed the morning. I barely met the pushup requirement of thirty, but I passed. I fared better on the sit-ups; I didn't "wow" anyone, but I held my own with a respectable forty in one minute. The 300-meter sprint flew by in less than fifty seconds, well ahead of the minimum time. All that remained was the 1.5 mile run. I had to run in under ten minutes and thirty seconds to achieve the necessary total points to pass the physical fitness test. I had to make up for my weakness in the other events with a strong run.

Out of all physical activities, running is what I know best. I flew around the track in just over ten minutes, and audibly "wowed" the agents who administered the test. By my former running standards, ten minutes to cover a mile and half was not fast at all. I had run two full miles in the same ten minute period when I had tried out for the Texas A&M cross country team, which I failed to make. But that had been ten years prior, so I was happy with my result. I had passed the physical exam. For corporate "desk jockeys" like me, the test was not a breeze, but for younger applicants with military experience, I would expect that this test would be a simple. I was happy with my result, one step closer to becoming an agent.

I took the entire day off from my corporate job, and after physical testing in the morning, I had several hours to kill before my polygraph. I changed clothes and decided to relax and watch a movie at a nearby theater. My ego-inflated head could barely fit through those wide theater doors. I was extremely confident that I was going to be an agent and would pass the polygraph without a hitch. In fact, I was quite overconfident. The polygraph started at about 1:00 PM. I was in good spirits and felt that I would soon be past what I saw as a mere formality. Three hours later I realized how incredibly wrong I had been.

After I was strapped in a chair and hooked up with various sensors, the test began. Basically, the polygrapher asks the candidate a series of questions that can indicate, based on his or her physiological signs (breathing, sweating, and heart rate), if he or she is being truthful. The tests are not always accurate but generally are a good indicator of whether a person is being deceptive in his or her answers.

The polygrapher, a black female FBI agent in her 40s, was one of the smartest, toughest, and most menacing figures I had ever met. She was cordial, completely professional, but all business. That was her job, and she did it well.

After I was asked the same questions over and over, the polygrapher would leave the room and come back in with her brow furrowed. She truly seemed puzzled at the results, leading me to believe that the FBI was convinced that I was being extremely deceptive. At first I felt that she was pretending that the machine was broken, but behind the stern face she believed I was being honest, but as the afternoon went on, she stated categorically, "The machine seems to be working fine, and we keep getting the same results." The unspoken message I received was something along the lines of, "You are a liar! The FBI doesn't hire liars! How dare you walk in here and lie, lie, lie!"

I had never (and to this day have never) done any illegal drugs. Not even a drag on a marijuana cigarette. Sure, I loved watching Cheech and Chong with my dad, which served as my education on pot. I had been to enough concerts and festivals to know what pot looked and smelled like. But I had not ever even seen any harder drugs, except for what movies and television portrayed.

I was asked the same question over and over about whether I had ever done any illegal drugs, and I began to feel guilty. Could inhaling secondhand smoke from another aisle at a concert be considered doing drugs? What else could possibly be buried in my subconscious that was starting to arise and throw a major wrench in my plan of being an agent?

I stood by my answer. Despite an urge to respond with a sarcastic "yes," I seriously responded to the question about whether I was the Pope, which was a follow-up question when I denied doing drugs for the fourth time, with a simple but firm "No." The repeated questions continued. When pushed to the brink and feeling that the questions were being repeated just to irritate me, I finally stopped giving "yes" or "no" answers, and impatiently, forcefully, and with finality said, "Look, I've never done any illegal drugs. Never. Maybe I am a strong person with convictions, maybe I'm just lucky that I hung out with the right crowd, or maybe both. But for whatever reason, I've never done any drugs, and if your test tells you otherwise, well, then your test is wrong."

After more than three hours of being strapped in the chair, the polygrapher unstrapped me and said I was free to go. I felt about as free as a person leaving a prison after a brutal beating from the other inmates. I felt guilty. Guilty as hell. I was almost ready to admit to anything that had even the most remote grain of truth. I wished that there was something in my past that I could admit to, but I was not about to start lying to the FBI just to please the polygrapher.

That was my first taste of why there could be valid legal challenges to confessions obtained during duress. I had led a sheltered life to that point. I had never known any cops or any real criminals. I believe that a person's rights throughout the legal process are of critical importance; in my opinion it is better to let one, ten, or even a thousand guilty persons go free than imprison one innocent person. Clearly depending on the mental state of someone who is given a polygraph test, a person could be tempted to admit to something, just to end the misery of the lengthy test.

Upon completion of the polygraph I began the most difficult phase of the entire FBI application process, which was simply waiting to see if I passed the polygraph. There was nothing I could do to help my odds. There was no preparation or training left to do. I kept painfully replaying how the polygrapher acted when she saw me out of the office. She was friendly and said I was "good to go," which really told me nothing. Each day I felt my chances of passing diminishing. After two weeks I began calling the FBI office to see if they had results. Nothing.

In the meantime, I continued to live my life but was thinking about the FBI every second. I went to a party in my hometown of West, Texas, and saw numerous old friends who had heard I was "going to be an FBI agent." Since I was still awaiting my polygraph results, I knew that I might not have passed. Instead of relishing the moment, I felt like a new actor in a television show pilot that just found out the show might be cancelled.

Almost one painful and worrisome month after my polygraph test, I finally got the call. I had passed the polygraph test. And I almost fainted; I was ecstatic! I knew I was in good shape and had a clean background, so for all intents and purposes, deep down I knew at that point that I would live the dream of being an FBI agent.

CHAPTER 3

The End of Normalcy

The transition from a corporate job to working in the FBI was fast and furious; the logistics of moving and preparation for my new job were overwhelming. Agents are expected to completely change lives in as little as a week. The only promise agents get from the FBI as to where they will be sent is that they will not be coming back to the office in the city in which they applied; they will not be coming back to their hometowns. This is a cause of stress and worry that foreshadows life in the Bureau.

I kept quiet about my testing to become an agent. I did not want to damage my flourishing professional career if I did not get hired by the FBI. And of even more importance to me personally, I wanted to preserve my pride if I failed to become an agent. I knew that the saying, "the only guarantee of failure is not to try," but I did not want to advertise my failure if I were not selected by the FBI.

I took various vacation days to have time to make preparations for life in the FBI. In the meantime, I was more successful than ever with my corporate job. About the time I was invited to fly to Kansas City for the Phase 2 interview, I was awarded a lifetime achievement award, complete with cake, speeches, and attendance of the top management of my company, including the CEO. I am a loyal person so I felt like I was being unfaithful. And in retrospect, despite the best wishes and ultimate acceptance and understanding of my decision to pursue the FBI career, to some extent I was right. I will always feel a small pang of guilt when thinking about the wonderful people at my former workplace, the same way that someone might feel bad about breaking up with the perfect mate who has been nothing but good to him or her. Only now in hindsight do I recognize how much I enjoyed my coworkers, and that overall the quality of my former corporate workplace was top notch.

After passing my Phase 2 testing and receiving my conditional appointment, I knew the time had come to tell my company that I was leaving. I spoke to my boss, who was completely accepting and understanding. I spoke with numerous other managers and employees, including the two who reported to me, and everyone was extremely positive. There was lots of hand-shaking and a general recognition that I was going on to serve a greater purpose and calling. The people at my company, including the CEO, could not have been more supportive. They allowed me to continue to work indefinitely until I went into the FBI, whether that was one month or one year. I will never forget these people who supported me with my dream.

The months drug on, through testing, through medical reviews, and through the background check. Aside from my job, my personal life needed significant attention. I was in the process of finalizing my divorce (which did raise a few questions from the FBI), and was an owner of a motocross bike, a boat, and a house, all items which for practical purposes I needed to get rid of before heading to the FBI Academy. It is no small task to get rid of possessions and rearrange a life in such a short and uncertain timeframe.

In November of 2005, I received final word that my background investigation had been approved, and that there were no more hurdles to entering the FBI Academy. From the online community, I had learned that at this point most people had to wait several months before entering the FBI Academy, so I expected to have several months to get my affairs in order. I put my house up for sale. I sold my boat. I sold my motorcycle. I made arrangements with my mother to store my other possessions. I was thankful that I did not have a spouse or children to worry about through this difficult transition period. Once again, this was a preview of how life would be in the FBI.

Only a few weeks after learning that I had made it through the entire pre-Academy processes, I received another call saying that I needed to report to the FBI Academy in two weeks. The report date was on a Sunday, and counting backwards, including travel time, I had nine days to wrap up my old corporate life. The call came right after Thanksgiving. I was elated. And I was terrified.

An incredible whirlwind of activity ensued. I gave my company a one-week notice of my departure. I accepted an offer for the sale of my home, and attended the closing the day before heading to Quantico. I worked furiously on moving possessions out of my house. I bought clothes and supplies for my upcoming FBI Academy experience.

Along the way, I managed to fall in love. There does seem to be truth in the phrase that you find love when you least expect it. I had been separated from my ex-wife for some time, and had recently finalized my divorce. I was not interested in establishing a romantic a relationship before heading to the FBI. In fact, I was specifically determined not to begin a relationship. But I found the perfect woman for me, Jennifer, and I could not help acting on what I knew would result in a lifetime of happiness. The chance to become an FBI agent was a lifelong dream, and a gift. But meeting my future wife was a much greater gift. People achieve happiness in different ways. For me, true happiness comes from a happy home life; a job, no matter how satisfying, is only "icing on the cake." Ultimately, knowing this helped me move on from my career in the FBI. But I don't want to get ahead of myself; at that point I had many exciting adventures awaiting me in the FBI.

So on Friday, December 9, 2005, on my nephew's second birthday and the day before what would have been my father's sixty-first birthday, I began the drive from Texas to Virginia. I took my time, enjoyed being on the road, felt relief that I had managed to get all of my affairs in order, and felt excitement that is difficult to explain. A lifelong dream was about to be fulfilled. Driving through the snow-covered Virginia landscape, I felt like a great explorer heading out to make discoveries. I was indeed on a journey that would prove to be enlightening and change my world.

CHAPTER 4

Welcome to Quantico

The first time I drove onto the Marine Corps base at Quantico, Virginia, I had images from *Silence of the Lambs* flashing before me. The forested rolling hills were dotted with snow patches. They were beautiful yet ominous. After driving several miles onto the base, after passing through a heavily guarded checkpoint, and after seeing ammunition depots and firing ranges, the harshness of my new home brought the serious reality of my endeavor to light.

I finally saw the sign pointing to a side road for the FBI Academy. The FBI seal further enforced the gravity of the journey I was about to take. After another thorough check was made of my identity, I was allowed to drive onto the FBI Academy grounds. I spotted more firing ranges. A sign pointed to the new FBI lab. I pulled into a parking lot, where I saw other vehicles that held occupants who shared the "deer in the headlights" look with me. I killed the engine in my truck. I had arrived. It was show time, and I felt like a terrified actor attempting his first performance.

I had preconceived notions that every action might be watched while I was at the Academy. Every situation could be a test. I thought there might be hidden cameras and microphones watching my every move. Evaluating me. Deciding if I was a worthy agent candidate. This compounded my fear and stress level.

A woman wearing khaki pants and a blue polo shirt with the wording "FBI Academy" greeted me. She was also wearing a holster with a blue plastic gun, which would become known simply as "blue handles." She was almost overly friendly and asked if I wanted help with my bags. I felt important driving to the Academy. But once I was there I knew I was at the bottom of the food chain. I was a true freshman. And a freshman getting help from an upperclassman, especially on a cold Sunday afternoon, set off alarm bells on all levels. Were new agents expected to work seven days a week? Would I be mopping floors? Cleaning restrooms with a toothbrush? I wanted to turn around and leave. Panic and terror waves pounded me. Fight or flight instinct kicked in. But I had quit my job, sold my house, and had nothing to go back to. Flight was not an option. I had dozens of friends and family who were counting on me to become an FBI agent. So going forward with my fight was the only choice. My dream was already feeling like a nightmare, and I had not even signed in.

Prior to arriving, I had filled out my stacks of pre-employment paperwork thoroughly. After signing in, I was immediately handed a huge stack of papers to complete. To my surprise, these papers were similar to what I had filled out before. Some were exactly the same. But that did not matter, because they wanted the "latest" forms, and the forms that I had previously filled out, which were sent by the FBI's human resources area, were not always current or complete. As a person with significant business process improvement experience, I had more alarm bells ringing. It was evident that the FBI is not immune to government inefficiency.

After gathering my bags, the New Agent Trainee, referred to as a NAT (each letter pronounced separately, not pronounced like the name of an insect) who originally greeted me showed me to my room. It was a cold and sparsely appointed dorm room, exactly like a college dorm room. Two suites connected sharing a single toilet and shower, with two sinks. There was minimal closet space. There were two beds with meager sheets and blankets. I had experienced living in a dorm in college and had never desired to return to those living conditions. But here I was, with five months of dorm life staring at me. Only I knew this dorm life was not going to be fun. No freedom to skip class and read a book by the lake. No pinball games at the student union. No television allowed in the room. This was more like a children's boarding school than like a college. The type of boarding school operated by tough, ruler-wielding nuns. The corner of my mouth revealed a small grin when I thought of the phrase "nuns with guns." My sense of humor would serve me well in making it through the difficult upcoming months.

Next came a tour of the facilities. Firing ranges. The gymnasium. Workout mats. Boxing gear. More firing ranges. A large lap swimming pool. The hall of honor, dedicated to fallen FBI agents. A library. The cafeteria. And yes, a building with some actual classrooms. I actually did look forward to class. Learning real crime scene investigation techniques while getting paid sounded like heaven to me; I could not imagine a better way to make a living. I figured that if I focused on the positives and things that I enjoyed, my attitude could carry me forward above any negatives that I would experience with my new profession.

The President of the United States, George W. Bush, happened to be visiting the Academy that day. He was working out, either running or bike riding, and used the same locker room that I would come to know intimately. I began to feel more excitement and pride, and I truly began to overcome my initial fear. I envisioned myself as being a kid who is starting school at Hogwarts as depicted in the *Harry Potter* movies. I felt a little like Harry Potter. Well, perhaps a little more like Ron Weasly.

Being so far from home was going to be a huge adjustment. I prayed that my cell phone would be in range and would be a life-line back to my world of "muggles." After powering on the phone, I was elated to physically locate a spot that showed one bar of coverage on my cell phone display. This was not a strong signal but at least was a signal. I called my girlfriend and future wife, and I was able to talk to her. This gave me incredible comfort. We discussed how we would see each other in two short weeks, and we agreed that I should make the most of my experience and try to enjoy living my dream. Just knowing that I would be able to easily call out made a world of difference in my attitude. I would have to do without my computer and television for the first time in my life, but at least I was not completely cut off from the outside world.

After I unpacked my belongings, my roommate, Justin, showed up. Initially he was quiet. He was younger than I was. He would become a lifelong friend. My suitemates showed up, and both were from Texas. I began to feel like I had allies, and I could tell that we were all experiencing the same emotions. This also gave me comfort. I knew that I could survive with the group. One of our counselors, a remarkable agent named Tom, who was approaching retirement, gave us the slogan "start together, finish together." This motto served our class well, because without the benefit of group dynamics, I would have never finished the first week. This was a valuable lesson, which broadly helps all agents achieve the FBI mission. Teamwork is paramount, whether it involves sharing intelligence, planning an investigation, or executing an arrest.

All of the NATs, numbering a total of thirty people, including three women, were assembled that first Sunday evening in one of the classrooms. Present were the class counselors, Tom, and Mary, a phenomenal agent who struck fear in our hearts, yet would fight for what was best for us, and was without a doubt one of the FBI's finest. Mary would demonstrate a tough love for the group, which I came to appreciate and respect. She would go on to head up the FBI lab's Chemical, Biological, Radiological, and Nuclear Sciences Unit, which serves a critical function in protecting the safety of the citizens of the United States.

Each student stood up and gave a brief summary of who he or she was, what he or she had previously done in his or her career, and why he or she joined the FBI. The makeup of the class revealed a number of former law enforcement and military members. This is reflected throughout the culture of the FBI.

The fact that neither military nor law enforcement experience was in my background would prove to be detrimental during in my time at Quantico and in the field, at least to some degree. There were also former attorneys, language experts, and engineers. One of the women, Lyla, who was in her late 20s, was an engineer and had no previous military or law enforcement experience. Although I did not feel like I would be the strongest member of the class, I knew that my road would not be as challenging for me as some of the others like Lyla. This also gave me a guilty sense of comfort, the same way that a member of the herd knows that there is a weaker animal in the pack, and knows that the weakest will fall victim first. Who would turn out to be the strongest of the group was impossible to predict; by the time we reached graduation, many of the non-law enforcement or military background NATs turned out to be some of the best agents, including Lyla.

When it was my turn to address the class, I stated that I had always dreamed of being in the FBI, and that with the death of my father, I realized that life is short and I must follow my dreams. While my statement was a cliché, it was true and genuine, as were the other NATs' reasons for joining. Upon conclusion of the evening, I knew that I was in the presence of the finest group of individuals I had ever seen assembled in one location. I knew that the FBI agent is truly an American treasure, and while I was scared and unsure if I could do the job, I was proud to be in the same room as people of this caliber.

CHAPTER 5

A Rude Awakening

The introductory day at Quantico was a mixture of fear, pride, and discovery. The introductory week at Quantico could be described in the same way. Except for the pride and discovery part. And sprinkle in some pain. And a feeling of suspended time. In summary, the first week proved to be fearful, painful, and never-ending.

On the second day, the alarm went off early. Sleeping in a new bed with a stranger in my room, with four men trying to shower, shave, and go to the bathroom at the same time is an interesting feat that I had last navigated ten years earlier in college. We all dressed up in our business clothes and prepared to take the photo that would go on our permanent credentials as FBI agents. After a meager breakfast at the cafeteria, we ventured to the photo studio in Hogan's Alley, the mock city used for training.

The tour of Hogan's Alley reminded me of touring Universal Studios. The sets were built by Hollywood set designers, and merely seeing Hogan's Alley was one of the highlights of my stay at Quantico. Getting shot numerous times by extremely painful paint guns in Hogan's Alley ranked toward the bottom of my experiences, but overall I have fond memories of Hogan's Alley exercises. The Hogan's Alley sandwich shop actually served food. There were residences, a hotel, a bank, and an industrial area. Our photos were taken in a building resembling a movie theater, which seemed appropriate.

We then ventured to the FBI Academy store to buy our khaki

pants, also known as 5-11's. These are utility cargo pants, a staple of FBI gear. Throughout the Academy experience, these pants are worn on the firing range, during exercises, and in the classroom. Originally designed for rock-climbers, these are some tough pants. We also purchased the blue polo shirts embroidered with the words "FBI Academy." I felt relieved to put these clothes on for the first time, because we then visibly were able to blend in with other students who had already spent anywhere from two weeks to five months in Quantico.

The remainder of the first full classroom day was filled with administrative items. The adrenaline rush from arriving at the FBI Academy the day before was replaced by tiredness and even some boredom. This was a welcomed relief, because I knew I could easily survive five months of boredom. But the boredom ceased on that first full day; the following day, Tuesday, December 13, would be forever etched in my mind as one of the most difficult and physically painful days in my life.

This was the day that our class took our first physical fitness test, or PFT, one in which each student had to pass the fitness standards set by the FBI, including pushups, sit-ups, a 300 meter sprint, and a 1.5 mile run. The running events were easy. I thought I was fit enough for the pushup and sit-ups with plenty of capacity to spare. But I was wrong about the pushups.

We went outside in the thirty degree, sleeting weather. Pushups were done on a freezing paved road, with a rough surface. Some students were yelled at for wearing non-FBI approved outdoor gear. We quickly learned that it is the FBI way or the highway. That included a ban on wearing personal outdoor weather gear rather than standard FBI-issued clothes. Did this make sense? No. Was this reasonable? No. Were the instructors being completely unreasonable assholes? Yes. I thought to myself, "Welcome to the FBI!"

The pushups required perfect form. Several defensive tactics instructors were tagged with evaluating agents and counting each person's pushups. These instructors were straight out of movies depicting the most sadistic drill sergeants I had ever seen. In what seemed to be a simple intimidation tactic, they refused to count perfectly executed pushups. It became apparent that my ability to do around thirty five pushups (versus a required thirty) might not be enough. I wound up with twenty seven pushups that counted, with six or seven that they did not allow due to incorrect form. Every pushup felt identical and perfect to me. Regardless, I had failed the test. That meant trouble. I knew I was suddenly one of the weaklings being separated from the herd. Mandatory "make-up" 6:00 a.m. workout sessions would be required for the next six weeks. Losing a couple of hours of sleep nightly would only add to the intense exhaustion I would feel each day.

I sailed through the running events and got enough total points to pass the minimum allowed for all events, so in my mind I had "barely" failed. But as would be explained to me by Deputy Director Lee Aspen, agents who had failed were effectively the scum of the earth. Failures. Rejects. Why had we even bothered to show up and disgrace the institution of the FBI? Interestingly, Aspen left shortly afterwards for a lucrative career in hotel security in Las Vegas; I had the feeling his presence would not be missed by the FBI.

After the physical fitness test (PFT), which was witnessed by FBI Academy faculty and counselors, the day was far from over. I had completely exerted myself during the test; therefore, I kept my fingers crossed that the remaining afternoon hours would be spent with a classroom lecture. Instead, we went into the gym, which I came to equate with a torture chamber. I became acquainted with knuckle pushups that afternoon. These were done in the same manner as normal pushups, except instead of using the palms of our hands, we had to use bare knuckles on a hardwood floor. The FBI instructors offered plenty of yelling and screaming, which provided the perfect audio track to a setting of complete misery. Phrases were yelled, such as, "The people of America don't care that you are in pain," and "The exit is right over there." I had completed seven marathons and had pushed my body to accomplish difficult feats such as winning 5K and 10K races. I could take physical pain. But I had never experienced anything like this verbal harassment and intimidation.

Since I had completely exerted myself during the PFT, I did not have much left in the tank for additional pushups. But that was all we did. Knuckle pushups. Over and over. We would hold ourselves up for minutes at a time, arms extended, with only our knuckles and toes contacting the ground. I went beyond what I believed was physically possible. I heard "UP, SELLERS!" screamed many times, since I could be identified by my name, stenciled on the back of my grey workout shirt. I was trembling with pain and exhaustion. I felt like a trapped, cornered animal. My knuckles began to bleed as we continued to do pushups for hours. The thin layer of skin that separated my knuckle bones from the hardwood floor was now gone; only some blood and torn soft tissue remained. The pain was beyond description. I felt sick but kept on going for several hours until class was over. The hours seemed to last for days.

Now that I had finished with my first afternoon of physical abuse at the FBI Academy, I figured that anything else would be a walk in the park. Much to my disappointment, my first firearms class proved to be nearly as challenging and intimidating. I had grown up with guns. I had even been grazed by an accidental discharge of a twelve gauge shotgun when I was younger, so I already had a high level of respect for guns and the potential hazards that are associated with them. I was comfortable with guns, which I thought would give me an edge over my classmates. The former law enforcement and military NATs had a degree of built-in respect from the firearms instructors, and with good reason. The firearms instructors, much like the DT instructors, also seemed to be straight out of a bad 1980s war flick. They yelled. And yelled. And yelled some more. They made me scared to touch a gun. They initially destroyed the confidence I previously had in handling guns. I had hoped that I would find enjoyment in firearms, which took up a significant amount of the curriculum's time, but I realized that firearms, in particular with the ice cold conditions that would have us laying in the snow for four hours during class at the outdoor firing ranges, would be only marginally more enjoyable than the horrific DT classes.

I was emotionally and physically torn down each of those days during the first week. In private, I was literally whimpering with misery, like a scared child who has been scolded and beaten. I am not proud of it, but that is how I felt. The classroom was the only area that I remotely enjoyed. Interviewing and interrogating, legal matters, and computer classes seemed like familiar territory. The classes were not easy, nor were they relaxing. But the demands of the classes were reasonable, and I felt they were directly related to skills that would be useful as an FBI agent. Unfortunately, the classroom would take up a far smaller portion of my total time at Quantico than I hoped.

The first week, which lasted from Sunday through Saturday, seemed to last for a year. The cafeteria food, the military style training, and the cold combined to create an almost indescribably miserable environment. I realized that I was only at the beginning. In comparison to a twenty-six-mile marathon, I had only finished mile one. Mile twenty-six seemed impossible to attain. After all of the celebratory feelings I had experienced prior to passing through the gates at the FBI Academy, this was indeed a rude awakening to life in the FBI.

CHAPTER 6

Finding a Routine

The first week was terrible, and the following few weeks were horrific. This was during the December holidays, so we were allowed to fly out of town for Christmas and New Year's Day. The high point of each week was hopping in my truck and driving off the Marine Corps base. Not only did that signify the end of a dreadful week, but it also ended the feeling of being cut off from the rest of the world. Even merging with the busy I-95 Interstate traffic made me feel happy and connected, which under most other circumstances would have only made me impatient and irritated.

The physical and emotional torture continued during the second week. I was so sore that I could barely move. I felt like I had been in a two-week-long brawl. As I left Quantico for my first weekend to be spent away from the Academy, I felt proud that I had accomplished surviving the first two weeks.

I flew to Michigan to visit Jennifer and her family, and felt a whole level of confidence that I had never felt before. In order to get a rental car discount, I sang karaoke. I had never done that in my life, but now I did not care. I was a proud FBI agent in training. I actually sang two songs and enjoyed it, but judging the faces of the rental car employees, I wisely elected to stop singing to give their ears a rest. I got engaged that long Christmas weekend, and shared my personal and professional excitement with my new future in-laws. It was a perfectly wonderful white Christmas, and I was optimistic that I would really make it as an agent. I was amazed at how my spirits had lifted.

Unfortunately the journey back to Quantico quickly brought on the opposite set of emotions. The cold, dark drive back onto the Quantico base became something I considered to be a "drive of doom," with each moment taking me closer to the place of misery called the FBI Academy.

As the weeks crept by, I took advantage of nearly every weekend to meet my fiancé in Washington, DC. I settled into the routine of surviving each day, and at the end of the day I would walk from the dorms to the empty classroom areas and would call Jennifer to chat. Afterwards I would study for my classroom courses, would return to my room, and then would fall asleep for six hours until I heard my suitemate's alarm go off. Each day passed very slowly, but each day was one day closer to the weekend. My classmates got a kick out of how I would sprint to my truck after we had completed our final task for the week at the Academy. I lived for those weekends as if I had held my breath for an entire week and could finally inhale at 5:00 p.m. on Fridays.

The weekends in Washington DC were wonderful, especially when contrasted with each week of experiences at the Academy. I enjoyed museums, restaurants, and movies with Jennifer, truly recharging my depleted emotional and physical batteries. History, government, and politics came alive through my repeated exposure to the DC culture. We usually stayed at Crystal City, which was convenient to the airport, the FBI Academy, and the subway. My drive past the Pentagon was always a sobering reminder of the dangers of the world we live in, and the importance of the FBI's mission in preventing terrorist attacks on American soil.

Over the weeks bonds grew strong with fellow agents. Groups would meet at the end of the day to go for a run through the wooded Virginia countryside, on some of the same trails that were used for filming *Silence of the Lambs*. Meals were shared in the cafeteria. Time slowly passed, and after four weeks a new class of agents arrived. I was happy to help these new agents with their bags and to give them a tour of the facilities. The new agents looked terrified. I was glad for their sake that that they had no idea of how rough their early weeks at the Academy would be. I had started to adjust to the shock of being at the FBI Academy and embraced routine as a way to mindlessly pass the time until I would graduate.

CHAPTER 7

Firearms

One of the great privileges of becoming an FBI agent -- and an equally great burden -- is the fact that every agent will carry a gun for his or her job. Tremendous resources are dedicated to training FBI agents in how to use their weapons. Thousands and thousands of rounds of ammunition and hundreds of hours of time are invested so that a NAT will be a firearms expert upon graduation.

At the beginning of the FBI Academy experience, NATs are forced to run around "naked" since they do not have leather holsters and the plastic guns commonly referred to as "blue handles." One of the first milestones at the Academy is agents' receiving their holsters and plastic guns, at which point NATs finally no longer stand out as being the freshmen of the FBI Academy. Throughout the instruction at the Academy, students receive additional pieces of gear and corresponding training, including bullet-proof vests, handcuffs, mirrors, and flashlights. NATs that are near graduation can be identified by their Batman-like utility belt appearance.

Firearms instruction at the FBI is not limited exclusively to doing target practice on a shooting range. Some time is also devoted to educating students on the dangers and the reality of carrying a gun, with the possibility of being in a firefight. This exposure introduces agents to the reality of their job, helps weed out agents who are not up to the task, and teaches agents always to fight for their lives.

Agents are shown a variety of videos that are not circulated outside of law enforcement. These videos depict police officers and subjects who get in real life gun battles. These eerie pieces of footage, typically captured by police car dashboard cameras or surveillance cameras, demonstrate how quickly someone's life can change. NATs view horrific scenes showing officers having their guns taken from them and being shot. Sobering images of police officers who have been killed in the line of duty are a grim reminder of the reality of the dangers inherent to law enforcement. And even more sobering are the images showing law enforcement officers who are severely physically maimed and live every day with a reminder of the sacrifice they have given for the safety of citizens of this country. Some of the images were beyond what is seen in a horror movie. These are the images that stick with the viewer for life and help form the instinctual situational awareness that is so important for law enforcement officers.

NATs learn to use FBI weapons, with the primary focus on the 40-caliber Glock 22. In addition, agents are trained on using shotguns and MP5 machine guns. While I never was faced with a situation in which I needed to fire my weapon at an adversary, I did have numerous occasions in which I had my gun drawn, and my training kicked in so that my gun-handling actions were on auto-pilot. During my career I had to handle my Glock as well as shotguns and MP5s in arrest situations, so the firearms training was definitely relevant to skills that agents would need in the field.

The firearms instructors are only one step above defensive tactics instructors with regards to their people skills (or lack thereof). Agents do not want to be on the bad side of the firearms instructor, especially the screaming and yelling type. Unfortunately I managed to have a former Marine gunnery sergeant as my instructor, and this person decided that I needed extra attention and yelling to make sure that I was doing what I should be doing. As previously mentioned, I was comfortable with firearms, and was used to firing an assortment of shotguns and rifles and handguns. However, the FBI has its own very specific way of doing things, which is an adjustment for the trainee, especially those who may have picked up bad gun handling habits prior to joining the FBI. Perhaps I was initially too relaxed around guns, and the instructor saw that I needed to have my attention more sharply focused on the task at hand. Believe me, my attention was laser-focused after being screamed at multiple times.

The firearms instruction included significant time devoted to firearms maintenance and cleaning. After every firearms session, weapons were torn down and cleaned thoroughly according to the FBI's standard method. Instructors strolled around the room and pressured NATs to clean weapons quickly. After being cleaned, guns were inspected, and if they had not been cleaned properly, the student received a stern lecture in front of the class and had to re-clean his or her weapon.

Before ever firing a weapon on the range, students are drilled in safety procedures. Students must recall safety rules instantly and know these rules by heart. The safety rules were always strictly enforced, especially in the gun cleaning room. I later learned of a specific incident that had contributed to increased emphasis placed on safety during the cleaning process (and not just safety on the firing range). Approximately two years before my time at the Academy, an instructor had an accidental gun discharge in the gun cleaning room, resulting in the shooting of a student. Fortunately, the student did not die, but he lost large quantities of blood and was saved only because of a trained paramedic being one of the NATs in the room at that moment.

There were other stories of fingers that had been shot off by NATs who did not hold their weapons properly. Luckily, there were no stories of NATs who were killed, but the FBI Academy was not immune to deaths of agents in training. Shortly before I entered the Academy, Special Agent Robert Hardesty was killed in a Hostage Rescue Team (HRT, the elite "super SWAT" team of the FBI) training accident. He fell twenty feet from an airplane wing, and he fought for his life for eight days at a hospital before succumbing to severe injuries. He was an experienced agent, and his death was a grim reminder of the dangers that can be present during a training exercise. Each FBI class picks a fallen FBI agent to learn about and dedicate our training efforts to, and SA Hardesty was selected by our class. After I graduated from the FBI and was a field agent, on December 6, 2006, FBI agents were informed of another death from a training accident. Supervisory Special Agent Gregory J. Rahoi, a member of the HRT, was killed in a live fire exercise. Clearly the need for safety was evident for inexperienced NATs, since even some of the FBI's most seasoned and experienced agents had lost their lives while in training at the Academy.

As the winter wore on, the cold weather made firearms classes even less enjoyable than usual. Temperatures were commonly below freezing, with thick layers of snow on the ground. Students were not allowed to wear gloves while firing, so for up to four hours at a time NATs were forced to lie in the snow while holding a literally freezing cold gun in their cold bare hands. Topped off with yelling and the pressure from the firearms instructors, this did not make for an enjoyable classroom recipe.

Over time our class came to see that some of our instructors did have a sense of humor and tried to make the class as much fun as possible. Some of our instructors were minor celebrities, including Olympic caliber pistol experts and former pro football players. Over time this made the painful firearms sessions more interesting and fun, and as the weather warmed and the instructors had more trust in the students, firearms became a tolerable class that I no longer dreaded.

Before a NAT can graduate, he or she must take a firearms test on which he or she achieves an 80% success rate on two of three practice target shoots. This test comes at the end of a NATs time at the Academy, and the pressure to pass the test is tremendous. If a NAT fails, he or she has to fall back to the next class and receive remedial firearms instruction. Repeated failings result in dismissal from the FBI Academy.

As my class reached the ending of our training and tested our firearms skills, one student did not successfully complete the firearms test. His graduation was delayed for four weeks. That may not sound like a long time, but that is an eternity at the FBI Academy. I managed to shoot well, scoring in the 90% range on my pistol qualification course, which included a total of 50 shots from varying distances in positions from 75 feet or as close as 5 feet from the target. This is not an easy feat, and despite my confident attitude and estimation that I was a good shot prior to entering the FBI Academy, their method of shooting truly did teach me to shoot much better than before I arrived. And more importantly, I learned to be even more confident and situationally aware of my environment. I learned to truly respect the responsibilities and potential consequences that come with carrying a firearm. The resources (in time and money) spent on firearms training for new agents is significant, but it is an absolute necessity.

CHAPTER 8

Defensive Tactics

When envisioning life at the FBI, I saw a montage of sharply dressed agents firing handguns at targets, smart people raising their hands excitedly in a classroom, and agents running and working together on an obstacle course in the woods, with an inspirational soundtrack thrown in for dramatic effect. I had not contemplated the hours that would be spent learning to physically fight and to arrest and handle criminals, but these skills were the focus of the FBI defensive tactics courses. Defensive tactics, known simply as DT, haunted everyone in the class throughout our stay at the Academy; even the toughest former cops and Marines dreaded each DT session.

The DT instruction sessions typically consisted of numerous knuckle pushups (which I still have scars from), boxing matches, and wrestling matches. Our instructor, an extremely physically talented but emotionless man named Roy Flaleligan, relished demonstrating both defensive and offensive tactics. He loved using members of the class as examples of how to execute painful defensive moves, and I was one of his favorite "involuntary volunteers." Neck twists, arm twists, takedowns, and non-compliant handcuffing demonstrations were frequent, only adding to my soreness and exhaustion.

While the DT instructors seemed like mean-spirited individuals, they were admittedly damned good instructors. They believed in their mission of training FBI agents to be ready for anything, and they knew that the training could save our lives. Tough love does not get any tougher than that at the FBI

Academy. While I personally feel that the DT instruction was overdone and unnecessarily difficult, I was never faced with a situation in which I needed to rely on my DT skills. Perhaps I am like a child who is mad at his or her parents for having to brush his teeth and not eat sweets. The child never develops cavities, and later in life, he realizes that his parents did him a favor. I can only imagine that if I had been suddenly placed in a life or death situation in which my survival depended on a few seconds of defensive tactics, I would be thankful for every second of painful training that I endured.

Seven weeks after the horrible experience of the first physical fitness test, which was part of the overall DT program, I had reached a second opportunity to take the test. I had been working out at 6:00 a.m., three times a week, in addition to attending DT classes. I was thankful that my roommate, who handily passed the first PFT, to support and encourage me to keep going, joined me for the morning workouts. I was always exhausted, but I was whipping myself into great shape. However, similar to my first PFT test, on the second test I floundered while doing pushups. My form while doing pushups broke down and was shaky, and the head of the FBI's DT instructors noticed. I was approaching the required thirty pushups, but suddenly the instructors starting disqualifying my pushups. I seemed to be stuck at twenty nine, but I had no gas left in the tank. I had already pushed myself to the brink, but I mustered up one final attempt at reaching pushup number thirty. I lowered myself down, and with every ounce of mental and physical strength I could summon, I pressed up while trying to hold acceptable pushup form. My muscles were completely depleted. My nerves were telling my brain that doing this last pushup simply would not be possible, but nevertheless my brain sent back orders to make it happen, no matter how painful or how long it took. The observing DT instructor allowed my last pushup to count, even though the form must have looked shaky at best and took me almost ten seconds to do. He saw that I had put forth a 100% effort, which I believe tipped the balance in my favor and allowed me to pass. This particular instructor demonstrated the first glimmer of humanity I had seen while participating in DT classes.

He pulled me aside and said, "You don't want to be mediocre, do you?"

"No, sir."

"I'll let that last one count, but I want to see you keep working on this."

"Yes, sir. Thank you, sir."

My happiness in passing the fitness test was second only to graduating from the Academy. By accomplishing that one final pushup, my world went from miserable to tolerable. The pressure from instructors for the class to pass the class was off. I never have forgotten that one instructor who showed me kindness, and any time I feel faced with a challenge to improve myself, I replay his words and ask myself if I want to be mediocre (sometimes the answer is "yes," but I still find his words motivating). To this day, thinking about that moment almost brings tears to my eyes, because it was the turning point at which I knew that I could survive the FBI Academy. I had learned how far I could push myself. I had hit an emotional and physical bottom but had made my first real steps in an upward direction.

CHAPTER 9

Bull-in-the-Ring

Time at the Academy seemed to be marked by a different rite of passage every week. These rituals are the traditions of the FBI, which all agents, both present and past, experience. These intense bonding experiences include fitness tests, orders night, firearms qualifications, exams, and ultimately, graduation. While conversing after the Phase 2 exam that I took to become an agent myself, one of the agents who had administered the exam was commenting on the brutality of a practice still in place at the Academy. According to her, people walked away bloody and with broken limbs. She called it bull-in-the-ring. I never forgot her comments, and as I began to hear mention of these words from my Defensive Tactics (DT) instructor, my stomach dropped as though I were dangling from a cliff.

Boxing is taught at the FBI Academy as part of the Defensive Tactics course. Participants do not learn the rules of boxing or strategies to win a match, but they do learn how to punch and how to fight. The culmination of this training is the bull-in-the-ring ceremony, in which based on his or her weight, the fighter will box five or six other agents. Each agent (the "bull") goes in a circle (or "ring"), boxing each opponent agent for thirty seconds. In other words, every agent gets pummeled for a total of at least three minutes, with a fresh sparring partner every thirty seconds. And of course the agent has to be part of "the ring" in which other agents are "the bull." The time for this torture also equals approximately three minutes. In total, that is six minutes of going head to head with some of the biggest, toughest, and strongest opponents I could have ever imagined.

This event typically marks the midway point through the journey at the FBI Academy. Everyone in my class, including the larger and tougher NATs, was anxious to get past this event. But each week would pass, and our DT instructor would not seem to have any information. There were scheduling conflicts that lead to our bull-in-the-ring ceremony being delayed for several weeks. As luck would have it, the ceremony was delayed until the day before I was to be married.

Jennifer and I could scarcely stand to be apart. Without a doubt we knew that we wanted to be together forever, and although our engagement was short, we were eager to get married and start our new lives together. We found a date, March 25, 2006, that was only three weeks before I graduated, yet was towards the end of my FBI Academy training. I figured by that point I would be on "cruise control" and my Academy experience would be winding down. On Friday, March 24, after I got out of my Friday afternoon class, I planned to head to the Reagan National Airport, board a plane to Austin, and marry Jennifer the next morning. But I found myself, with less than twenty four hours before my wedding, strapping on boxing gloves and hoping that I would at least be conscious for my big day.

I am a big person. My large frame, with a height of 6'2", fills out with an average body type. I had once been an excellent runner, weighing around 170 pounds, but my weight was around 195 while at the Academy. I was not muscular, especially in my upper body, as evidenced by my limited pushup ability. Unfortunately, when the boxing groups were assigned, muscular build was not one of the factors considered. Prior career was not a factor. Height was not a factor. Only weight mattered. And I was towards the heavier end of the spectrum in my class. Sure enough, I was assigned to the heaviest division for boxing. My long "chicken legs" were not going to do me any good in the ring. Flight was not an option; I would have to fight.

Other groups had the smaller NATs, including the females in

the class. I hated sparring with the females in practice, because I had learned to "never hit a girl." However, the instructors ensured that these women experienced every bit of pain and suffering that the males did, including taking punches at full force. For the bull-in-the-ring ceremony, I would have been grateful to punch a girl a few times if that meant that the force returned on me was not as much as the larger males could deliver. But the groups were split up to ensure some degree of fairness would be achieved for the sparring partners.

The other boxers in my group were all former military or law enforcement members. There was an extremely muscular former Sacramento police officer, and an even more muscular agent who was formerly with the New York Police Department. Another former cop from Buffalo, New York, was also in the group. A former Marine and a former Army soldier rounded out the group, along with me, a former corporate business process improvement and IT manager. My fellow boxers were not the least bit intimidated by me; I wished I could have shared the same sentiment about them.

With the theme from Rocky blaring (this time not in my mind, but literally, the music was blasting from the speakers in the rafters), most of the faculty at the Academy entered the gymnasium. All of my instructors were there to wish us the best of luck beating the hell out of each other. All eyes were on my group, which had the heavyweights.

The DT instructors made it clear that everyone was to go all out, with 100% effort, 100% of the time. Any perception of a lack of effort would result in starting over from scratch. Nobody wanted to box more than he or she had to, so you could bet every punch would be thrown with maximum force. These were agents who had been mostly pent up at the Academy for fourteen weeks. Sometimes in close quarters, tensions flare. This was the release point for all of the numerous frustrations that life at Quantico had developed. I couldn't help but feel like I was in prison, and felt I was about to "become someone's bitch."

The ring formed, and I felt fortunate to be the fourth person in the ring. I did not want to go first, because everyone would be most rested and ready to deliver the most powerful blows. In a situation like that, participants tend to look for the silver linings.

The whistle blew, and the first "bull" began boxing person number one in the ring. There was no strategic dancing around maneuvers allowed by the boxers. Fists were immediately flying, and it looked like a scene from the final moments before the bell rings to end a boxing round. But this was just the beginning. My nerves built as I saw the "bull" make his way every thirty seconds to the next person. A short whistle signaled that it was my turn to start swinging.

The next thirty seconds were a blur. I fought my instinct to curl up in a defensive position, or better yet, a fetal position. I tried to block and duck, but also found the resolve to connect every blow that I could, with as much power as possible. I found that my opponents went into a mixture of offense and defensive moves, which gave me some hope that I could hold my own. Of course, my opponent had boxed three people immediately before me and was already getting tired, but just the fact that I could offer a few well-aimed punches that required blocking was encouraging.

Finally the whistle chirped again, and the "bull" went to the next fighter. My first thirty seconds (out of six minutes) was done. I was still standing. My relief reminded me of my motocross racing days when my nerves would be almost unbearable before the starting gate dropped, but after making it to the first corner, my anxiety disappeared and I could enjoy the race. I was able largely to turn off my nerves when boxing, only trying to stay focused.

My encounters with the next two boxers were uneventful, if one can consider an all-out thirty second brawl with former cops uneventful. Then came the long whistle that ushered me into the center of the ring. For the next three minutes, I would become the "bull."

I started strong and did my best. The first thirty seconds were tolerable, just as my previous bouts had been. But when boxing person number two in the ring, I could already feel my arms getting sluggish. My punches connected but were not doing any damage. My defensive reaction times were slowing. A few punches that I could tell were powerful connected full force with my head. I truly felt like a punching bag. There was nothing to do except to keep fighting. As I fought each heavyweight NAT through successive whistle chirps, making my way one by one around the ring, I felt a wave of sickness. My energy level was completely depleted, and I only wanted to try to protect my head. But the DT instructors were screaming to keep punching, and I sure as hell was not going to risk starting over with person one in the ring. I had to keep swinging, and I did. Although I had almost no strength left, going on the attack was the best way to prevent getting continuously pummeled.

Finally, the long whistle blew, signaling the end of my role as the bull. I had survived an excruciatingly long three minutes and was still standing. I still had two more thirty second bouts with the next "bulls," but my primary moment of pain was over. I boxed my last opponents and purged my remaining strength and my frustrations. After finishing the final boxer, I was spent in every sense of the word. As I removed my boxing gloves, I thought that if I never put on another pair, I could live the rest of my life a happy man. To this day, not one time have I put on boxing gloves. And I am a supremely happy man.

Much to the delight of my heavyweight bull-in-the-ring companions, I wound up with one teardrop shaped bruise on the corner of my eye, which was easily fixed with some makeup. I was able to fly out that night for Austin as planned. My wedding and associated photos were perfect. I was not sure if I was happier to be married to the woman I loved or to be done with the bull-in-the-ring experience, but regardless, that was one of the happiest weekends of my life.

CHAPTER 10

Pepper Spray

The physical challenges presented at the FBI Academy were memorable. Time spent in the classroom was greater than time spent in Defensive Tactics, but the painful memories of DT are the ones that have stuck with me. Aside from bull-in-the-ring, there are other DT milestones that must be passed to graduate from the FBI Academy. One of those, the "pepper spray day," is one of the worst experiences at the Academy.

Why does the FBI subject agents to pepper spray? Because there is always a chance that an agent could be sprayed while on the job. A criminal could easily be armed with pepper spray, and our training was designed to provide direct experience in that arena, which could eventually mean the difference between life and death in a worst-case scenario. But I also can imagine that part of the reason is so that a few sadistic FBI instructors can enjoy watching the students, whom they appear to despise, experience additional physical misery in addition to the usual days of bloody knuckle torture.

I was fortunate to be at the FBI Academy during winter months, which naturally brought cold weather. For enduring pepper spray, colder is better. My class was sprayed near the end of our term in late March 2005. The day was cool and crisp, and for once I felt that the conditions were ideal (unlike conditions for the firearms or knuckle pushups that I had done in the snow).

Our class donned our workout clothes, and with some joking around, trudged outside to begin our afternoon of blinding pepper spray fun. Our DT instructor was present and was assisted by the other DT instructors. In addition, a small group of faculty members (FBI agents) were present to watch the activities. Much like the bull-in-the-ring experience, FBI agents are not immune from the car-wreck syndrome; they absolutely must turn their heads to sneak a peek at the carnage. My classmates and I were less than thrilled to be playing the role of the carnage.

The class split into pairs, with one agent being sprayed in the face with pepper spray, and the other agent acting as a subject (or "bad guy"), who would be apprehended by the agent who had just been sprayed. After the instructor was satisfied that the drill had gone correctly, the okay would be given and the agent who had been sprayed would be led away to a water hose to rinse pepper spray residue from his or her eyes. My roommate and I paired up and took a position midway through the line that awaited the blast to the eyes law-enforcement grade pepper spray. We began to watch the misery of our fellow agents unfold.

The first candidate was sprayed in his eyes and a reddish-orange circle appeared on his face where the spray was applied. I could tell that there was a slight sense of enjoyment from the defensive tactics instructor as he had a slight grin while doing his job of inflicting pain on the agents. The first sacrificial lamb clearly was in pain. Using his fingers, he forcibly pried opened one of his eyes and a completely red and watery eyeball was revealed. As instructed, the agent pulled out his plastic blue-handled gun, located his partner (playing the role of a subject to be arrested), and issued the commands: "Get down on your knees," and "Don't move!" The instructor was satisfied with his performance. He was then mercifully led away by his partner to the watering hoses, shuffling along, obviously experiencing intense physical pain to his face and eyes.

The cycle continued as each person endured the horror of a direct application of pepper spray for approximately two minutes per cycle. With each person getting closer I realized that

I had underestimated the power of pepper spray. There is a reason that law enforcement, including the FBI, utilizes such a powerful chemical weapon. Although pepper spray is just an organic product made of ground peppers, the pain inflicted by the spray feels like the worst concoction that a mad scientist could create in a laboratory. Pepper spray is simply designed to incapacitate the intended recipient in a non-lethal manner.

After I watched a number of other agents go through what was obviously a horrific experience, it was finally my turn to stand in front of my classmates and instructors and receive a healthy application of pepper spray directly to my eyes. I heard the hissing sound from the canister and next experienced a tingling sensation on my face. For about two seconds I thought that the pain might be tolerable. But within three seconds I felt like I had planted my face in a fire-ant mound. The burning sensation was indescribable; I had never felt such intense pain on my face and eyes. My instinct was urgent and powerful: make it go away. I wanted to head straight for the water hoses. But if I wanted to graduate from the Academy and become an agent, I had no choice but to continue the task at hand.

After the initial blast of spray, the instructor forced me to wait about ten seconds before arresting my subject. Ten seconds turned into ten years. I was finally allowed to try to locate the subject and begin apprehending him. I was able to force my eyes, which resembled tiny cat-like slits, open, and located the position of the subject. I tried my best to issue verbal arrest commands to this person. The sounds that came from my mouth sounded garbled and were difficult to understand. But I pressed on, held my ground, and tried my best to firmly command the subject. Finally the instructor gave the verbal acknowledgement that I had successfully completed my portion of the pepper spray exercise. My roommate quickly ushered me away to the awaiting watering hoses, where I desperately sought relief.

I flushed my eyes for several minutes, but like a clogged toilet, just flushing with more water could not wash away the problem. At least the water was cold and soothing, and provided temporary relief. However, there were only five watering hoses for our class of thirty individuals. As the final NATs received their application of pepper spray, everyone crowded around the water hoses. After cycling back through the line several times to have access to water, my eyes began to feel slightly better, and I was able to leave them open for a few seconds at a time.

But despite my level of misery, I was one of the fortunate ones. Some other NATs clearly reacted worse to the pepper spray than I did. One NAT was still experiencing eye pain several days after the event. The misery that FBI agents voluntarily endure is evidence of the dedication and sacrifice they make for the sake of our country. The pain is far beyond the comprehension of most people. I considered myself to be able to handle pain stoically. I almost liked the pain associated with running a marathon, or holding my breath under water (which I could do for more than three minutes). But the intense pain that goes with feeling like a flame has been applied to your eyeball, or the pain associated with knuckle bones grinding through the skin for hours at a time, is not something that most people can imagine without experiencing.

I would have loved to sprint back into the FBI gym's locker room and stand under the cold water of the expansive shower facilities. Unfortunately, the FBI Academy had just issued a warning that the lockers in the gym had been contaminated with PCBs (Polychlorinated Biphenyls, a harmful chemical substance linked to a variety of health issues). The problem was so severe that the lockers were chained off, and all possessions in the lockers were lost (including watches, clothing, and shoes). The showers in the locker area were also closed, which meant that showers to wash off the pepper spray had to be taken back in the dorm rooms. With only one shower per four students, the demand for cold water was high after the pepper spray event. I impatiently awaited my turn to get in the shower to wash away the remaining pepper spray residue, and finally was given my turn for full-body relief.

I thought that I would be back to normal after washing with soap in the shower. However, despite my best efforts, there still remained traces of pepper spray on my clothing and in other areas that made the following few days extremely uncomfortable. I soon discovered that other areas of my body, aside from my face, were even more sensitive than my eyes to the effects of pepper spray.

At least the event was over, and I knew that much like the other events agents had to endure, the entire FBI Academy experience would soon be ancient history. Only three weeks separated me from freedom, and much like a prisoner, I was thankful that my time was almost fully served. While I had entertained a daily fantasy of just walking out of the FBI Academy for good, my serious contemplations of escape began to fade. I knew that there were only a few more remaining hurdles to freedom, including academic tests, the firearms test, and team building event (hosted by the defensive tactics instructors). As I found to be a consistent pattern with the FBI in general, not knowing what was in store for each day was a blessing.

CHAPTER 11

Team Building, FBI Style

While the FBI is composed of an elite group of individuals, ultimately it is teamwork that accomplishes the mission of the FBI. Throughout my training, the concept of teamwork was heavily emphasized. One of the most enjoyable team building activities that I encountered was early on during my time at the FBI Academy. We spent a Saturday going to the United States Holocaust Memorial Museum in Washington, DC.

This museum offered a moving experience unlike anything else that I have ever seen. One of the worst chapters in human history is well-documented, with atrocities highlighted in ways that are disturbing, yet respectful to the millions of victims. I was already well versed on World War II history, but the museum unveiled a new realism and perspective for me that I will never forget.

All FBI classes had an opportunity to visit the museum as part of the curriculum at the FBI Academy. Despite all of the critical information we learned about criminal law, firearms, and defensive tactics, I feel that this day spent at the Holocaust Museum was the most valuable day of learning for future FBI agents. We learned about government-sponsored murder. We learned about what can happen when human rights are violated. We learned the dangers of the abuse of power of government. We learned about the horrors of massively scaled policing that were directed by a madman. We learned what happens when the people do not stand up to fight tyranny. We learned the important lessons that the FBI must always be careful always to pay attention to so that similar atrocious acts will not ever occur in the United States. The reinforcement of the dangers of too much power for the government only strengthened my belief that the FBI, while not perfect, is making the right efforts to ensure that future FBI agents approach their job, which entails a significant degree of power and trust, with responsibility, care, and hindsight gained from the awareness of the brutalities committed in the past.

I experienced an unexpected, unique form of a team building activity as part of my defensive tactics class. The event took place at the Marine base in Quantico, complete with a real military obstacle course used by the US Marines. Prior to the event, I knew that this class exercise would entail plenty of running. Running is my forte; I did not dread that part. But I knew that the event was organized by the defensive tactics instructors, which set off the alarm bells in my mind. In my corporate life, team building meant that employees would take the afternoon off for food, drinks, and an activity like bowling or laser-tag. I knew that this would not be the case for an FBI DT team-building event. Other NATs who had been in classes before mine were mysteriously tight-lipped about the event, which I knew spelled trouble.

Each NAT was issued a military-style helmet, and we boarded a bus that transported us to the site of our teambuilding exercise. As the class drove to the other side of the Marine Corps base, I heard bits of positive conversation and laughter, and I felt a general sense of enthusiasm. After all, this was one of the last major hurdles before our graduation, and the weather was a nice sunny, clear, warm, spring day in Virginia. The months of cold and snow and ice-freezing temperatures had disappeared, along with our remaining time at the Academy, and this was reflected in our high spirits.

After riding for about twenty minutes, I peered out of the bus windows and got my first glance at what the afternoon would hold in store. There was a fenced-in area with obstacles that were essentially giant puzzles. The obstacle consisted of different stations, each with a variety of wooden planks, massive pools of water, barrels, and other items. I anxiously awaited these challenges because I knew they would involve problem solving ability and teamwork to achieve. This seemed to be as close to an American gladiator type reality show as I would ever find. I thought for a few moments that the day might turn out to be as enjoyable as my corporate team building events.

The class exited the bus and awaited further instructions. The other DT instructors, along with our instructor, quickly began barking orders, telling us to hurry up, setting the tone for the day. I felt that this was largely for show and that an afternoon of running and doing obstacles and teambuilding exercises could still prove to be enjoyable, at least to some degree.

We were instructed to do a run for about forty-five minutes and then return to the team-building puzzles. After working on the puzzles for fifteen minutes, we would run for another forty-five minutes, and then work on yet another puzzle. The cycle would be repeated throughout the remainder of the day. Our instructor lined us up and then led us away on a run. I tried to soak in the warm fresh air and enjoy the moment. We ran for about a mile, and the instructor suddenly stopped us and started yelling for us to get down on our knuckles. Yes, this meant knuckle push-ups. My knuckles still had open wounds from the repeated knuckle push-up abuse in the gymnasium. My heart sank as I realize that the afternoon held more than just running and puzzle solving. The other instructors, who also ran with the group, assumed their usual roles of yelling and screaming and threatening, "If you don't do those push-ups correctly, the rest of the class will suffer while you watch." And as I had seen many times before, they meant it. The FBI's unwritten pro-hazing policy was in full force for the day.

After the pushups, the class continued to run for a few minutes, and then suddenly we were halted again. The instructor told us to get on our backs and began leading us through a series of leg-lifts. This exercise looked easy, like something practiced in an aerobics class. The participants simply lie on their backs, and move each leg up and down rapidly, without either leg touching the ground. But after hundreds cycles of up-and-down leg movement, it becomes extremely difficult. It was still very early in the afternoon, and I knew that my body was in for some serious torture before sundown.

We got back on our feet and continued the run, finally coming to some real military obstacles that the Marines used for training. The obstacles included rope bridges to traverse, wooden barricades to crawl over, barbed wire to crawl under, and pipes to crawl through. In a sense, I felt that I was on an adult-sized playground. Growing up, I had seen plenty of movies that depicted soldiers in training, which had always interested me and looked like fun. Although there were no flutes, bugles, or snare drums playing that day, I still enjoyed tackling these obstacles. This was living a childhood desire to play on the ultimate military playground. Despite being tired, I still managed to enjoy this part of the team-building event because I knew it was only going to last for one afternoon, and I mentally treated the experience as if I were in a fantasy military boot camp.

Some of my classmates did not fare as well as I did on the obstacle course. A female NAT approached the barbed wire obstacle, where agents were forced to lie on their bellies to crawl underneath the barbed wire. I had just made it through the obstacle, and being one of the first to arrive on foot at the obstacle, I chose a path that was dry and had no water to crawl through. Of four possible paths under the wire, two were mostly submerged, with thick layers of sludge in at the bottom. My classmate began to take one of the paths with water and mud; however, before getting down on her hands and knees to initiate the crawl, she noticed the dry paths. She hesitated and then she quickly shifted over one "lane" in order to avoid the standing cold water and mud. She made it almost halfway through underneath the barbed wire when our instructor began yelling at the top of his lungs for her to turn around. My classmate was puzzled, and did not seem to understand what was happening. She finally backed out of the obstacle and waited for further instructions. To no one's surprise except her own, she was ordered to crawl through the muddiest and sloppiest route. Our instructor had reached his last day of being able to exert his power over us. Clearly he intended to take full advantage of that and would continue to haze the NATs until the last minute of the last day that he could. The NAT made it through the sloppy, muddy route and emerged exhausted, tired, and upset. And the afternoon of fun was just getting started.

After approximately forty-five minutes of this combination of running and physical exercise, our instructor led us back towards the team-building puzzle area. First, he had the class stop at the pull-up bars, which was a weak spot for me physically. Every muscle in my body was already strained and tired, but I had to force myself to do as many pull-ups as possible keep from getting screamed at. We finally arrived at the stations with the giant puzzles and were given an opportunity to get a quick drink of water. Then for the next fifteen minutes, we were actually able to enjoy puzzle solving and teambuilding. After a brief set of instructions, our teams, which consisted of four to five agents, each tackled a separate puzzle. The puzzles required both intelligence and physical strength. The puzzles seemed impossible at first glance, but with creative thinking and effective teamwork, they could be solved. If an agent failed to solve them, there was no penalty, but if he or she did succeed, then he or she felt a true sense of camaraderie and accomplishment. If I did not have the pressure of angry DT instructors, this would have been an extremely enjoyable activity that I would have considered paying my own money to do. Repeating my technique that I had perfected since arriving at the FBI Academy, I shut the instructors out of my mind and enjoyed the moment.

The class repeated this vicious cycle three more times. We

ran up and down hills, did more knuckle push-ups, and performed more obstacle course activities. As the afternoon wore on, the puzzles became less fun, and the running and exercise portions began to be incredibly painful. Just one hour-long cycle of forty-five minutes of running and exercises followed by fifteen minutes of puzzle-solving would have been a great workout for even the fittest athlete. Four hours of this intense activity was nearly unbearable.

By the last session, many in the group were experiencing extreme muscle cramping that prevented them from being able to run. I was one of the best runners in our group, but nevertheless, my legs began to cramp the same way that they had at mile twenty of the marathons that I had previously run. Unlike a marathon, where only the leg muscles are completely exhausted, every muscle had reached the limit at which cramping and full shutdown ensues. A marathon is particularly rewarding, partly because it is voluntary, and the runner can quit at any point but keeps pushing to the end. However, the FBI's teambuilding day was not really optional, unless the agent in training wants to lose his or her job. There was a feeling of accomplishment after the teambuilding day, but there was also a feeling that I had been abused. People that have gone through the military are used to this type of treatment. But for me, despite an excellent running background, I did not adapt well to what amounted to physical abuse and hazing.

When the afternoon finally wrapped up, everyone was quiet. The bus ride back to the dorms was completely silent. Despite successfully completing the day, people were too physically and emotionally drained to want to converse. It had been a tough day for the class, and not one that people would remember fondly.

The experiences of that day were another way of ensuring that the candidates that emerge from the FBI Academy are dedicated and tough. The question on my mind that day was, "How tough do agents need to be?" I could not help but think that the failure of the FBI that helped allow for the 9-11 tragedy had nothing to do with military-style toughness of FBI agents. The FBI is made of extremely competent, dedicated people, but the culture is a blue-collar military and police mentality. Leadership comes from the ranks, which frequently means that forward-thinking people with significant cultural diversity and business knowledge are scarce and undervalued. The FBI's slow transformation to fighting terrorism, white collar, and cybercrime is no surprise, considering the mentality of the DT program at the FBI Academy. Again, I recognized the value of learning to defend myself against an assailant, but it was difficult to see the value of week after week of physical abuse that left permanent scars on my body.

CHAPTER 12

Academics

Sitting in a classroom and learning from the FBI instructors was my favorite part of the Academy experience. I enjoyed learning from the mostly fantastic FBI Academy instructors, who were also agents. Their knowledge and experience were incredible. And they were compassionate, could clearly remember their days as new agents, and realized the hell inflicted on NATs during firearms and DT classes. They had a sense of humor and would often show funny videos or tell corny jokes to the class. This part of the Academy was the most college-like and helped make the duration tolerable.

The opportunity to interact and ask questions of the instructors made me feel like a reporter who was granted with incredible insider's access to the FBI. I often found myself viewing my surroundings not as a participant, but more as a third party observer. I did get exposure to classified material, although the Academy does not exactly spill the nation's deepest and darkest secrets to NATs. But I did feel "in the know" and proud that my country had granted me this access.

A NAT undergoes a variety of classes, each with an examination, with a total of approximately ten exams. On each exam, a NAT must score an 85 or higher. Throughout the time at the Academy, a NAT is allowed only one opportunity to retake an exam. Scoring less than an 85 twice results in an automatic expulsion from the Academy. So once the NAT has used up his or her one chance for a retake, all future exams must be scored at 85 or higher, or the NAT is expelled. Scoring an 85 is not difficult on most of the exams, but there are reams of material that must be memorized. Passing an exam without proper preparation would be virtually impossible. Academics are not taken lightly at the FBI. Being at the FBI Academy is nothing like the training classes I have experienced in the business world, where attendance is practically a guarantee of passing the class, assuming there is an exam in the first place. FBI Academy classes are much more similar to university courses in which if the student does not learn the materials, he or she will not graduate.

An FBI agent is a federal law enforcement officer. Therefore, knowing how the law works is critical for an FBI agent to have to be effective in the field. A large block of time in legal training is spent on the Constitution and Constitutional amendments. This is important because the Constitution spells out how the legal process works at a high level and is the basis for the operation of our legal system. Much to my surprise, in both classroom training at the FBI and in the field, I found that the FBI is truly conscious of the rights of citizens and works very hard to make sure those rights are not infringed upon. This awareness of the rights of individuals goes back to the quality of the people within the FBI who are there because they want our country to be better, and they are the last group of people who want to see any of our rights eroded. Unfortunately, a dramatically different view of the FBI is held by many, including the American Civil Liberties Union. But both groups care deeply about rights of citizens, and I see no reason why there could not eventually be a working relation and even a partnership between the two organizations. I see both groups as having common interests, issues, and enemies.

Topics covered during legal instruction included how to write search warrants and arrest warrants, and when it is appropriate to pursue these legal mechanisms. We learned about reasonable doubt, probable cause, and the various levels of certainty required for the varying stages of the criminal legal process. We also learned how to advise people of their Miranda rights, which, of course, I had been exposed to through numerous movies and TV shows. I looked forward to the day when I would actually read someone his or her rights.

We learned about the differences between state and federal law, including how the different systems work and how the FBI interfaces with the United States attorneys. We were also taught how the FBI works with district attorneys within the states and the legal mechanisms that allow FBI agents to legally participate at the state level. This would be crucial information for me to learn, as I would eventually find myself working with state authorities on a daily basis.

Considerable time is spent on instruction of the FBI's deadly force policy. FBI agents are expected always to be armed while on duty, and although the goal during an FBI agent's career is never to use his or her weapon, the reality is that FBI agents are armed, and some will be confronted with situations in which they need to use their weapons. Over fifty FBI agents have lost their lives on the job, mostly in gun battles. And many more agents have been in dangerous situations that required them to use deadly force in order to protect their own lives. The FBI policy is clear: an FBI agent is never allowed to issue a warning shot. When an FBI agent pulls the trigger on his or her gun, the objective is always to eliminate a threat that poses an imminent danger of death or serious bodily harm to the agent or others. Agents are given numerous written scenarios and have to state whether deadly force is authorized, and why FBI policy does or does not allow for deadly force in a given situation.

This section of legal training, in combination with other aspects of training, brings home the reality that at any time FBI agents can be faced with having to use their guns to kill a person. Unlike a movie or television show with actors who go on living even if killed in a script, the FBI agent's job is real, and so are the consequences of killing a human being. To people who have not carried a weapon for a living, this may simply sound like a serious responsibility, but nothing more. However, the emotional and psychological impact for many, including me, cannot truly be comprehended without being in the position of an FBI agent, law enforcement officer, or armed member of the military. Many sleepless nights, filled with horrible shooting nightmares, are common to FBI agents. This fact is almost universally ignored by management, but in multiple private conversations with other agents I learned that this is a common occurrence. These unsettling dreams, which happened frequently while I was an agent, still occasionally haunt me.

The legal training we received was concluded with an event called moot court. Just three or four days before graduating, agents are exposed to a mock courtroom environment, complete with attorneys and a judge. The agents have to testify and are subjected to various tactics that they can expect to see in an actual functioning courtroom. Moot court is taken so seriously that if the NAT lies while on the stand or makes up facts or information while testifying, the agent will be expelled from the FBI Academy and will not graduate. This exact scenario has actually happened, and after enduring a very difficult training process, I cannot fathom how horrible it would have been to make it that far through the process and not have been allowed to become an FBI agent.

Significant time is devoted to learning interviewing and interrogation techniques. This training was similar to what I had envisioned before arriving at the FBI Academy. Agents are instructed on methods to elicit information from witnesses and subjects, or suspects, of investigations. Most of the techniques are intuitive. For example, if an agent is trying to get information from a witness, he or she wants to put the witness at ease while making sure that he or she asks all the right questions and gets all of the information that the witness knows. Open-ended questions are preferred to make sure witnesses share all of the information and details possible. When interrogating criminals, for example, suspected bank robbers, an agent should look for both verbal and non-verbal cues that the subjects are lying. Ultimately, to get a confession, the agent should be able to identify with the criminals and minimize the criminal activity that the subjects committed. If a suspected bank robber is captured and questioned, the agent might tell the robber that the agent understands that the robber only needed money, that the agent knows how bad the economy is, and that the agent can understand that the robber merely wanted to put food on the table for his or her family. The agent might tell the robber that in the same situation, he or she might have done the same thing. The reality is that most of these criminals simply rob banks because they are lazy and want to get money for drugs or alcohol, but blaring out the unpalatable truth will typically result in tight-lipped subjects.

I thoroughly enjoyed learning about these techniques and practices, and I agreed with the instructor's comment that effective use of interviewing techniques and getting information from people is really at the core of an FBI agent's job. An effective interview can be the difference between a successful prosecution and a failed attempt. The ability to successfully converse with a subject could likely be the most effective way of identifying and preventing the next major terrorist attack. Time spent doing knuckle pushups did not seem useful to my job, but learning how to get information from people seemed to be an invaluable investment, and continues to benefit me in all aspects of life.

The interrogation techniques were frequently tested in a practical environment. NATs practiced their skills by being given a scenario, followed by a face-to-face physical interview with a paid actor or actress. Throughout the interview, students' actions were monitored and recorded, and NATs were required to write up and report the results of the interviews using interrogations in a standard reporting form called an FD 302. I would go on to write hundreds of 302's during my time in the FBI. The actors and actresses really seemed to enjoy their roles, resulting in an extremely effective hands-on learning environment. These exercises were beneficial in instructing me in how to present myself as an FBI agent, how to get information, and how to accurately document the information. When I became on operational FBI agent, I found myself using my knowledge gained from my interviewing and interrogation classes on a daily basis.

Another topic at the FBI Academy was forensics, which was another area that I had expected to study in great detail. Unfortunately, this area did not receive as much attention as I would have liked, but I certainly enjoyed the limited classroom time and practical activities for this knowledge area. Other areas of forensic related instruction including learning how to do surveillance and evidence photography, how to preserve blood evidence, how to conduct a search, how to lift fingerprints from objects, and how to fingerprint subjects. This was truly enjoyable; my interest in this area was largely the reason that I desired to become an FBI agent.

NATs also have limited coursework in learning about terrorism. In my opinion this instruction was lacking, not due to individual fault of the instructors, but due to time limitations of the established curriculum. With a total investment of just a few hours, we quickly breezed over the various terrorist factions and groups worldwide, and what their motivations are. I realize that much of the FBI's terrorism training is specific and conducted on the job, but clearly, more emphasis, especially after 9/11, should be placed in this area. Not surprisingly, I feel that the hours spent doing knuckle pushups would have been more useful learning about terrorism. I have a feeling that most American taxpayers who fund the FBI would agree.

One of the more interesting coursework areas, and another topic that most people associate with the FBI, was instruction in counterintelligence topics. Within the intelligence community, this is known as tradecraft. This subject fuels the imagination of writers of spy and espionage movies. Along with many others who grew up watching James Bond, I fantasized about being a spy or some type of secret agent, and this was the part of my instruction that got me closest to that fantasy. Special spy gadgets along with a treasure trove of true spy stories were shared with the class. With the cold war era gone, there rightfully is not as much emphasis placed on this topic as in the past, but for pure entertainment value I would have been happy to spend more hours learning about the fascinating world of espionage, double agents, and spies.

There is also significant coursework in operational case management duties. How to conduct an investigation, how to navigate through the mountains of forms and stacks of paperwork, and knowledge of the approvals and authorizations that agents must have for each investigative techniques is taught. This is covered through the sharing of real-life examples taught by FBI agent instructors. The real-life content and examples proved to be interesting and made the expected administrative steps palatable. Of course, this side of being an FBI agent is never depicted in film or books, since it would be min-numbing to audiences and readers.

Unfortunately, the FBI also forces agents to take what I consider ridiculous coursework that reminded me of the corporate world that I was so happy to leave. We endured a computer based training class that everyone in my class concluded was a complete waste of time. The class was supposed to teach agents how to think. Clearly, FBI agents do not just show up at the FBI Academy without knowing how to think. At least the NATs were given an opportunity to formally provide feedback on the course; my hope is that a slew of negative comments will change the curriculum to remove this course and instead spend time on other issues, such as national security and terrorism.

Other areas of academic training that I did not feel were adequately covered are cyber-crime and white collar crime. In today's environment, there should be instruction specific to mortgage fraud, internet scams, and corporate fraud. Unfortunately, these topics are largely ignored. While much of the training for agents is on-the-job, emphasis on the country's greatest criminal and security threats should be made up front during an agent's stay at the FBI Academy.

Despite a few shortcomings, overall the FBI Academy's academic training is thorough and in my opinion does an adequate job of preparing agents to be effective on day one when they arrive in their first field office.

CHAPTER 13

Orders Night

What field office will an agent be assigned to upon graduation from the FBI Academy? Unless an agent is from New York or Los Angeles, he or she will not be returning to the field office that he or she applied through. That meant that San Antonio and the satellite offices, including Austin, were off limits to me. So where did I want to go? Where did I think I could go? All agents would discover their location fate about six weeks into the FBI training program in a ceremony called "orders night."

One of the first tasks assigned to agents is the ranking of their field office location preferences, which would be a factor in the FBI's determining of each agent's first office of assignment. There are fifty-six FBI field offices, all which had to be ranked from 1 to 56. Depending on the needs of the Bureau, agents are assigned to an office that attempts to take into account their wishes, but with absolutely no guarantees.

Within the FBI there are abundant rumors and speculation regarding the best way to approach the mysterious orders assignment process. Some classmates simply ranked the field offices in their order of preference as they were asked to do; they took the process at face value. But the majority of us pored over any and all reports and statistics we could get our hands on to make an intelligent and strategic ranking decision. And of course we all tried to take into account the reputation and other factors of the field offices. This was no easy task since we were all new to the FBI.

The first realization when ranking the offices was that

although there are fifty-six field offices, there are hundreds of satellite offices, called Resident Agencies (or RAs), that are considered to be part of those field offices. The impact of this is more dramatic in more sparsely populated geographic areas. For example, the Dallas office has ten satellite offices, ranging in locations across north and east Texas, from Tyler to Lubbock. So if an agent is assigned to the Dallas office, he or she might head to work every day with an exciting view of the Dallas skyline, and be looking forward to heading to a Cowboys game on the weekend. Alternatively, an agent could be assigned to the Dallas office, but to the Lubbock RA. Lubbock is a fine city, but unless an agent is used to wide open spaces and minimal nightlife, he or she could be in for a big culture shock. Agents have to keep in mind the impact of this on family. This is one of the many sacrifices that FBI agents make that people take for granted. This is the reality of being an FBI agent.

By looking at historical trends and current staff excesses and shortfalls, one could predict the field offices that people would be sent to. For example, New York had a reputation of having high staffing needs, largely because living expenses are significant (despite a cost of living adjustment). So in a new class of agents, one could speculate that a couple of agents would be pulled to go to New York, even if New York was not ranked at the top of the list by any agents.The remedy for this was to rank undesirable field offices at the bottom of the list, even if there were other locations that would be preferable. I ranked New York last. I would rather have gone to New York than many other locations, but I knew if my ranking of New York was lower than others, I would not have to go. In summary, I felt the best strategy was to try to identify the field offices that would need people, and rank those accordingly.

I utilized the same strategy to get where I wanted to go. Ideally I would have loved to head to the Dallas field office, which is close to friends and family. But at that time they had a full staff level, and that the odds were nobody would be going to Dallas from my class. I ranked it towards the top but reserved the top spot for a city that I thought that the FBI realistically would be sending agents to. After much deliberation and consultation with Jennifer, we chose San Diego as number one.

Even getting assigned to the San Diego field office was something of a long shot. I did not put any other offices in the top ten that I thought anyone would have a realistic chance of going to. And San Diego was risky because there were two RA's for San Diego, which mean that living in San Diego was far from guaranteed. There was North County, which is between San Diego and Los Angeles. The waiting list to transfer to North County was significant within the San Diego office, due to the coastal location and desirable surroundings. And then there was the El Centro office. El Centro became famous in the 1970s when a gunman entered the FBI office and shot and killed two agents. The office is small, with about a dozen agents. The territory they cover includes most of the southern California border, from the Colorado River to the edge of San Diego County. El Centro agents work mostly drug and alien smuggling case, which I knew would be a gritty, dirty, and dangerous business. El Centro is hot and dusty, and the type of city that, if a person is passing through, he or she should would probably avoid stopping unless there was a fuel or bathroom emergency.

After waiting for six weeks, orders night finally arrived. The tradition is for all agents to be handed an envelope in which they state the office they have ranked as their top location preference, followed by the they have been assigned to go to. The city is noted with a pin on a map, showing geographically where all class members will be headed upon graduation.

My roommate Justin had taken the advice of the group that explained how to rank the cities. Their recommendation was that if an agent wanted to go to a specific geographic area, then rank all of the offices in that area at the top of the list. For example, if an agent wanted to head to southern California, he or she should rank Los Angeles, San Diego, Phoenix, Sacramento, and San Francisco at the top of the list. However, agents really needed to ask themselves if they really could be happy living in any of those cities. For example, San Francisco is vastly different than Los Angeles, both geographically and culturally. If an agent put both cities on his or her list, he or she would have to be sure he or she would be happy in either location.

Justin wanted to stay in the Midwest. He was from Chicago and had played wide receiver at Michigan State University. His friends and family primarily resided in the Great Lakes region. He ranked his list based on that. Number fourteen on his list was Buffalo, New York. Previous classes were typically getting their top ten picks. Occasionally someone would be awarded a pick in their thirties, but that seemed to be unlikely.

The orders ceremony began. Students and teachers, including our firearms instructors who suddenly transformed into ordinary, personable people, crowded into a small room with great anticipation. Pizza was doled out, although appetites were almost nonexistent; all agents were deep in thought (and prayer) about where they might wind up. The envelopes arrived, and the ceremony began.

As agents opened their envelopes and announced their assignments, the trend of getting assigned to favorable locations looked good. All agents were getting their top ten picks. Several people got their number one picks. Justin's turn came up. Facing the class, he opened his envelope. His face turned a ghostly white, and he announced "Buffalo" as his office of assignment. He trudged back to our table and was genuinely depressed.

Many agents ranked San Diego towards the top of their list, but only two of us had San Diego as number one. The other person was one of the female agents, a tiny but physically and emotionally powerful woman named Stacy. She was the smallest agent in the class, and clearly was at a disadvantage when wrestling with men twice her size in our DT classes. But she gained a great deal of respect because she was tough and never quit, and on top of that was one of the smartest and most likeable students. I knew that she had San Diego as number one, so if she did not get San Diego, I most definitely would not.

After opening her enveloped, with an unsure smile she announced "Los Angeles" as her office of assignment. San Diego seemed off the table for me.

Finally it was my turn. I was extremely nervous, but in an excited way. My future was at stake. My home. My life. As I opened the envelope in front of my audience, I could hardly believe my good fortune. Printed on the sheet was "San Diego." I announced San Diego, everyone clapped, and I settled back in my chair with an extreme sense of relief. I figured I just needed to just endure my remaining time at Quantico, and then could spend my career in sunny San Diego, enjoying life as an FBI agent during the week, with fun on the beach on the weekends.

In the following weeks, my assignment was conveyed to the San Diego office. The San Diego office reached back out to my supervisor with my first squad assignment. I was assigned to a VCMO, pronounced "Vic-Mo," squad, which stands for Violent Crimes and Major Offenders. With my years of computer and white collar business experience, I was shocked at my assignment. I had a sinking feeling, knowing that that type of work would not be a good fit for my personality or my family life. But the FBI clearly states that all agents are assigned based on "the needs of the Bureau." I could not understand the logic of my assignment, but I was not in a position to argue. My feeling of elation had turned to dread. With a risk-averse personality, the uncertainty of a violent crime squad assignment loomed over me like a dark cloud.

CHAPTER 14

Hogan's Alley

Simulations of the wide variety of duties that FBI agents execute were conducted through training exercises at the famous Hogan's Alley complex at the FBI Academy. Various activities including surveillance, arrests, and searches were performed. These exercises often resulted in bruises and painful situations, but also provided some of the best stories and funniest memories. A screw-up at Hogan's Alley would be remembered for the duration of our stay at the Academy. And the real life scenarios that were presented still ring in my head to this day. Situational awareness is key to safety, whether arresting someone or buying gas at a convenience store. The skills honed at Hogan's Alley were the most critical with regards to an FBI agent's safety.

One memorable occasion in Hogan's Alley was a day when the class was using live paintball guns, which were modified Glocks; these were not the guns that shoot the large "bubble gum" paintballs used by the public for recreation. The overall objective for the class was to clear out a building filled with armed subjects. Paid actors played the parts of subjects, and they clearly enjoyed inflicting pain on the New Agent Trainees.

My group of several agents entered the building, which was dark and required use of flashlights. There were hidden compartments quite similar to what a person would see in a haunted house. I was shot on two occasions, with one leaving a permanent minor cosmetic blemish to the skin on my back. The agent in charge of the training exercise doubled over with laughter at my reaction to being shot, and went on to tell a story about my "Academy Award winning performance to getting shot" to future classes. It was all in good fun, and despite some physical pain, this experience was enjoyable and resulted in extremely valuable knowledge for agents. To this day I approach dimly lit stairways and corners with caution, and still can crack a smile at the fun that I had in Hogan's Alley.

Other training scenarios involved people who were suicidal. Still others involved driving up on police officer shootings. Other scenarios had agents being carjacked unexpectedly. In Hogan's Alley agents never knew what would happen, and anything and everything did. The FBI did a great job of showing agents everything that can go wrong, and helped us prepare for all types of situations.

The final exercise in Hogan's Alley involved wrapping up a fictitious case that pieced together details from previous classroom exercises. The class was able to arrest our classroom "bad guy" subject, Billy Ray Hankins, who we also jokingly referred to as Billy Ray Cyrus. From wiring up cooperating witnesses, to surveillance, to searches, to arrests, to bank robberies, to vehicle stops, Hogan's Alley was truly a learning environment and playground for law enforcement. This final arrest scenario showed the class how all of the pieces fit together and was a satisfying conclusion to an effective chapter of training for new agents.

CHAPTER 15

Graduation

One of the things that I came to appreciate during my stay at the FBI Academy was the visibility and accessibility of senior management, including the head of the FBI. The FBI director, Robert Mueller, made several appearances and visited my class and others while I was at the Academy. Remember, this is the guy who had a daily meeting with the President of United States, and ultimately was responsible for all criminal and terrorist investigations in the United States. He was an extremely busy man, but he made time for us. When visiting our classroom, he asked how things were going for us. He also stopped by the cafeteria a couple of times and visited with students. And most importantly to me, he attended my graduation day, he addressed the class and audience, and he personally handed each agent his or her credentials. He took time to chat and pose with all families for pictures. I viewed this as a demonstration of true leadership. I have a great deal of respect for Mueller, and I feel that he brought a level of integrity and change to the FBI that was painful internally and criticized externally, but was the best anybody could have possibly done in that role, especially considering he assumed the helm of the FBI one week before 9/11.

Other agency officials in general were accessible and seemed to really care about the students. Administrators, instructors, staff, and the agent faculty were always available to students to help them with their problems. Our counselors for the class, including Supervisory Special Agent Mary Ebert, and Special

Agent Tom Elfman, were two of the finest agents in the Bureau and dedicated eighteen weeks (and weekends) of time, effort, and energy to producing a successful batch of students. They were excellent role models, and they lead by example. They showed the class that they were willing to sacrifice their personal lives for the sake of the class. Similar behind-the-scenes efforts are commonplace in the FBI.

After eighteen long weeks, graduation day finally arrived. Jennifer met me the weekend before graduation, and we booked a hotel for her to stay in near Quantico until I graduated. I received special permission from my FBI counselors to stay off the grounds of the FBI Academy so that I could be with my new wife. My counselors may never know how much that gesture meant to me. In a sense, I felt that I graduated the week before when I was finally free to live outside of that FBI dorm. My roommate and suitemates were great, but none of us enjoyed living in a dorm situation. The stark contrast of living with my wife, even in a small hotel room, was absolute heaven.

My family flew to Washington, DC, and drove to Quantico to watch my graduation. My mother, brother, niece, nephew, and in-laws were in attendance. In a large auditorium setting, families were shown a video that summarized the experience and activities at the FBI Academy. While watching that video, I felt vastly relieved to be at the end of the training and not at the beginning. Then the time came for the agents to walk onto the stage to receive their credentials. One by one, agents strolled across the stage as their names were called. Each agent paused in the middle of the stage to shake hands with Director Mueller, a picture was taken, and then each agent exited the stage. On the surface it appeared similar to most college graduations, but the feeling I had was unlike anything I had ever experienced before. I thought that when I graduated as an industrial engineer from Texas A&M University, that would be my greatest lifetime accomplishment. But graduating from the FBI Academy and receiving my credentials from FBI Director Mueller surpassed that many times over. That day will always rank at the top of my list of favorite lifetime memories; I became the person that I thought I had always wanted to be. I did have a deep sadness that my father, Kenneth Sellers, was not able to witness this event, because I know he would have been amazed and proud. But I also knew that he was quite proud of me in my former pre-FBI life, and that was enough for me.

After the graduation ceremony was over, agents and family members gathered in the Hall of Honor, dedicated to FBI agents who have lost their lives in the line of duty. This was the last opportunity to say goodbye to my classmates, including my roommate and suitemates. It was a time for us to meet the family members of classmates that we had heard so much about. It was an incredibly happy occasion, but it signaled the end for spending time with people I had become so close to. I realized that this small group shared a special, intense bond that nobody else could ever understand. Almost like a group of people who were stranded on an island and finally rescued, nobody wanted to remain, yet goodbyes were difficult. I will never see most of these impressive, dedicated agents again, but they will always live fondly in my memory.

Finally it was time to make one last trek to the firearms area and permanently receive my Glock 22 handgun. As I walked to the armory to see my firearms instructor one last time, my sense of accomplishment and pride continued to swell. After receiving my weapon, I walked alone back to my truck, knowing I was done. Jennifer and I hopped in, I cranked the engine, and I pulled away from the FBI Academy one last time. I was leaving a place that I had grown to hate so much, but I could not help but smile and feel those same goose bumps that I had felt when I drove onto the FBI Academy grounds that first time so many months ago. It was like crossing the finish line of a marathon that after training and working so hard to finish. I felt the intense joy that the event was over, and I realized I had accomplished one the greatest feats I would ever attempt.

CHAPTER 16

Go West

Taxpayers can be assured that FBI funds are not spent wastefully. The FBI has a strict policy that governs an agent's move to his or her first office. New agents are allowed just five days to pack up all their belongings, sell their house, get their kids into schools, and get established in their new city. Agents are granted some limited travel time, but that evaporates quickly. The expectation that new agents can magically rearrange their lives in a week is completely unreasonable, in my opinion. However, I was thankful that I was no longer doing knuckle pushups or being yelled at by FBI instructors, so with the right perspective, the almost insurmountable task of moving across the country in a week seemed downright enjoyable. I focused on the fact that I was getting a "free cross-country driving vacation" from the FBI.

Jennifer and I headed west after my graduation and worked our way through the beautiful landscapes of the southeastern United States. We did stop for the weekend in Lexington, Virginia, and stayed at a rural one-room cottage. This was a gorgeous place to stay and was the first chance that I had to really spend some quality and quiet time with my new wife. It was sort of a mini-honeymoon; we knew that we wanted to go to France on our "official" honeymoon, but we also knew that would be in the distant future.

Those first few days after graduating from the FBI Academy were memorable in many ways. I carried the pride of finally being a full-fledged, real-life FBI agent. I at last had my credentials and my badge, with my trusty Glock strapped to my side. I remember my first stop at a fast food restaurant in Virginia. I felt powerful and important. I walked in thinking *Special Agent Sellers would like a cheeseburger, his wife will have a chicken sandwich, and by the way, have no fear because if there's any trouble just duck because I'm a gunslinger and can handle anything.* Thank goodness nothing bad happened, because despite my intense training, I was a completely green rookie not remotely prepared to be a law enforcement hero and save the day.

My brain did frequently switch gears from relaxing to thinking about the details of our pending move from Austin to San Diego. Fortunately, I had been able to sell my house in San Antonio before entering the FBI, but Jennifer and I now had a house in Austin that we needed to do something with. We needed to figure out what we could take to California, knowing that space would be extremely limited in the expensive city of San Diego. We had much to accomplish in a very short time.

After arriving back in Texas, we quickly inventoried our possessions and rented a U-Haul to move some items to my mother's house, located near West, Texas. We had to pack enough items in our own car so that we could survive in a hotel for a limited time while searching for a place to live. I knew that I would be starting work and would be dressing professionally as FBI agents do, so I had to pack a broad assortment of clothing ranging from informal shorts and t-shirts to dress pants, jackets, and ties. Jennifer quit her job at Dell, and we felt fortunate to be in a financial position in which we could afford to do that.

I cannot imagine how difficult the move would have been with children. Some newly-minted FBI families have to deal with the situation presented by the FBI by having one spouse stay behind with the children, while the other spouse moves to another city as an FBI agent until the family can be reunited. That would happen immediately after a new agent had spent months apart from his family while at the FBI Academy. This is nothing compared to the sacrifices that the men and women of the United States military make, but considering that an FBI agent is a career for civilians who frequently come from stable professional backgrounds, the sacrifices that FBI agents make should not be trivialized.

In our case, we had four animals including two Chinese pug dogs, and two long-haired Persian cats. To simplify our move, we decided that the cats could stay with my mother for a few weeks and that we would take our two dogs with us. Another logistical consideration was what to do with my full-sized Chevy truck. Aware of the expenses and parking challenges in California, and knowing that I would be provided a work car by the FBI, we decided to sell my truck.

After an intense three days of furiously packing, we set off for California. As we began to work our way west through the Texas hill country, I felt like Frodo or Bilbo from Middle Earth setting off on a great quest that would be filled with adventure. I had a sense of excitement, tempered with an underlying gritty knowledge of the profession I had chosen. It was getting close to show time for me as an FBI agent. There was no more training; it was time for the real deal. The bad guys would be real, and they would be firing real bullets. No whistles or instructors would stop the action in a tight spot. Expectations would be high. A small screw-up could result in immediately getting fired, a medium screw-up could mean the difference between life and death for me or others, and a major screw-up could have disastrous consequences for the FBI and for our country. The phrase, "Be careful what you ask for, because you just might get it," played through my head numerous times and seemed to be stuck on repeat the entire time that I served as an FBI agent. But overall I tried not to think negatively rather to enjoy each moment.

We had sunny skies, good tunes, and good times heading west. We took three days to drive to San Diego from Austin. We stopped overnight in El Paso and Tucson. Along the way we saw vast desert landscapes and stopped to see Saguaro National Park. It was enjoyable but could have been more fun if we did not have the uncertainty and stress awaiting us at the other end of the move.

Our hectic move to San Diego is more evidence that the life of FBI agents is best suited for people without significant others. In the 2007 movie *Breach*, which was filmed during my time at the FBI Academy, Laura Linney stars as an FBI supervisor over a terrorism squad that figures out that there is an internal mole who heads up the FBI's Soviet counterterrorism division. This true story is fascinating, and the movie is faithful to the facts with minimal artistic license. In the movie, the Laura Linney character, whom I would later meet in San Diego when she became the Assistant Special Agent in charge, was shown as having no personal life, being forced to eat TV dinners, without enough personal time or stability even to have a cat. This is an accurate depiction that is commonplace for many agents. However, at this early point in my FBI career, I was still optimistic that the FBI would be a good family organization, although I knew that my violent crime squad assignment was going to pose a challenge to that.

We finally entered the state of California and made our way across the desert floor, over the Colorado River, past the giant sand dunes, and along the Mexican border on Interstate 8 all the way to El Centro, California. As I had learned at the FBI Academy when ranking my desired cities to be assigned, El Centro is one of the satellite offices out of the main San Diego FBI office. Sometimes agents, including new ones, have the unlucky draw of being assigned to El Centro. El Centro resembled every other small border town that I had seen along the Mexican border. Signs of poverty were evident. As something of an outdoorsman and former motocross racer, I could have managed to be happy in El Centro by myself by riding in the sand dunes and exploring the desert, at least for a limited time. However, I imagined that the lack of luxurious grocery stores, the scarcity of restaurants, and the few entertainment options would have quickly eroded the small amount of enjoyment that El Centro could offer. I felt thankful that I had wound up in the city of San Diego, because if I had been assigned to the El Centro office, my wife and I would have felt confined and dissatisfied.

After a brief stop in El Centro, we began winding our way up through the mountain range that separates the desert from San Diego and the Pacific Ocean. The temperatures were cool, and elevation quickly rose from sea level up to 5000 feet. The mountains were pretty but not beautiful, displaying a rugged, arid quality. Trees were small and scrubby, and there were no waterfalls or rivers. When we finally arrived on the outskirts of San Diego, Interstate 8 widened to five or six lanes, and I began to feel like I was really in California. Palm trees became plentiful; the scenery continued to improve. We crossed over more hills, passed by the University of San Diego, and made our way into the Mission Valley area of San Diego where our hotel, Mission Valley Resort, was located. This hotel was one of the few that claimed to be pet friendly yet was somewhat affordable. The FBI did have a small travel allowance, but it did not quite cover our stay at the Mission Valley resort, which was really a 1950s style hotel, and was dated and somewhat rundown.

The beauty of San Diego exceeded our high expectations, revealing numerous hills and trees. We already loved it, without even having seen a beach. We familiarized ourselves with San Diego for the next couple of days and searched for apartments that were within a couple of miles of the beach. San Diego beaches are beautiful, although these areas tend to attract transient residents. Beach bums young and old are prevalent, and we had to ask ourselves if we were willing to tolerate this crowd along with unbelievably high prices, just to live near the beach. We finally decided that we really are not "beach people," and that we would not mind a fifteen minute drive to get to the ocean.

We finally settled on living in an area called Tierrasanta, known as "the island in the hills," which happened to be conveniently located across the Interstate from the San Diego main FBI office, which is where the majority of agents and squads in San Diego are based. I knew my initial assignment in San Diego would be working downtown in a small office, but I thought that it could not hurt being located somewhat close to the main office in case I was moved to another squad. We settled on an apartment complex that had a policy that allowed for two pets and had ample green grass, so we decided that our dogs would be happy there. Once the kitties arrived with my mother, who would visit in another month, we planned to keep them hidden; I did feel some guilt in being an FBI agent who was willing to be deceitful, even for something as harmless as going over the limit for the number of pets at an apartment. Not unlike most criminal minds, I was able to rationalize my behavior: FBI agents ultimately need to be practical and have common sense.

The apartments we settled on were attractive in appearance, but were older units, most without air conditioning. We paid an additional sum for air conditioning, which amounted to a window unit placed in a hole that was cut in the living room wall. This two bedroom apartment, with a size of approximately 700 square feet, cost $1700 per month. Clearly we were not in Texas anymore, where the same quality of accommodations would cost about half that amount.

We got moved in and tried to get settled. At that point our possessions consisted of only what we had packed in the car. We brought an air mattress, which we used as our bed for a few days. I had to start my job at the FBI before the movers arrived with our remaining possessions, including furniture and clothing. I am the type of person who likes to have everything in place and organized before I can really concentrate on anything else. It was difficult for me to start work knowing that my life at home was in a state of limbo. But the business of the FBI does not stop and wait for agents to get their personal lives arranged. Welcome to the San Diego FBI.

Part II

Adjusting to Life as a New Agent

CHAPTER 17

Street Agent Day One

My first day in the San Diego field office was Monday, May 1, 2006. I did not sleep well the night before; I was extremely nervous. I knew that my violent crime assignment would be dangerous and that the job could be all-consuming. This would prove to be an accurate prediction.

Jennifer dropped me off in front of the main FBI field office in San Diego at 8:00 a.m., and I approached the gate with my credentials in hand. A uniformed, armed guard at the entry point told me to wait, and then I was greeted by a friendly female agent, Special Agent Sarah Ely, who was about my age. She was warm and personable; I could tell that she could identify with the difficulties and anguish associated with an agent's first real day on the job. She introduced me to people and helped me get established with a new photo ID card, passwords, and equipment. With any job most individuals can expect to feel some apprehension when meeting new people and learning new things. The FBI experience is a highly magnified, intense version of a "first day at work."

When touring the main office, I learned about security protocols for the San Diego FBI Division, along with the location of the bathrooms, interview rooms, file rooms, squad areas, and the evidence room location. Little did I know how many times I would frequent the evidence room in the coming months. I was issued an FBI car, commonly referred to a "bu-car," which stands for Bureau car. I quickly learned that the stereotype of the FBI driving American sedans proved to be true. The FBI parking lot was packed with Crown Victorias, Suburbans, and other assorted American makes and models. My assigned car was a five-year-old Buick with nearly 100,000 miles on the odometer. The car had enough wear on it to make me wonder if the odometer had previously flipped the 100,000 mark and perhaps the car was 200,000 or even 300,000 miles old. The vehicle had no window tint, which gave me immediate concern about how I would be able to conduct surveillance. At first glance I was less than thrilled about my ride. However, once I climbed in and discovered how to turn on a completely dazzling assortment of colorful flashing strobe lights, a siren, and bullhorn, I was as excited as a five-year-old who just received his or her first bicycle.

After introductions, orientation, and processing at the main San Diego field office, it was time to head downtown to meet my new supervisor and squad mates. Much to my amazement, our downtown San Diego satellite office, located in an office building near the United States Attorney's office, did not have permanent parking spaces allocated to the FBI. So rather than parking in a location with immediate proximity to the office, we were issued a magnetic card which would allow us to park in a nearby mall parking garage. I learned that each morning I would have to park at the mall, walk through the mall, and then cross the street to my building. A fifteen story elevator ride and a few winding corridors later, I would finally be at my office. This amazed me, because depending on factors such as traffic, elevator availability, and available mall parking spots, ten minutes could easily pass before making it to a vehicle when responding to an urgent call, including in-progress bank robberies. This did not seem to be a brilliant idea for a location for the FBI's violent crime squad, where agents are expected to drop everything and immediately react when crimes occur.

However, I personally enjoyed being located in downtown San Diego and parking in a mall. Shops, waterfront eats, and places to walk and get fresh air were everywhere. This was my first experience working in a downtown environment, which was a pleasant change from the dull suburban corporate office parks that I had previously worked in.

My new supervisor, Supervisory Special Agent Harry Norris, was a young, vibrant, and practical agent whom I came to greatly respect and enjoy working for during my early days in the Bureau. Meeting SSA Norris for the first time, I explained that my household goods had not even reached San Diego. He told me that I had several more days to arrange my personal affairs as needed, and had an understanding that it is difficult to perform professionally when one's personal life is not in order. Immediately, I could see that the people on the front lines of the FBI in field offices have a human side and try to make an incredibly difficult job as manageable as possible. However, despite the best efforts of seasoned veterans in the FBI, I would soon find that working on an all-consuming violent crime squad would not mesh well with personal time or family life, despite my best attempts not to be pulled into a nearly 24/7 work schedule.

I was also introduced to my training agent, the person officially assigned to help mentor me as a new agent for my first two years in the FBI. This is the person that new agents can direct questions to, and they have responsibility to make sure that new agents gain relevant professional experiences. They also ensure that the new agent's experiences are recorded in a training manual to demonstrate successful on-the-job completion of a variety of basic skills that FBI agents need to possess. I was assigned to Special Agent Daniel Easton, who also served as the bank robbery coordinator for the FBI in the Southern California San Diego area. SA Easton had a fantastic range of experience through working eighteen years of cases, with many involving violent crime. I knew that I was in good company and that in any situation I would have an excellent support person to consult for advice and direction. Throughout the FBI, most experienced agents are compassionate, understanding, and helpful by nature and prove to be invaluable assets for new agents.

I met the other members of my squad throughout the day as they trickled in from performing various investigative actives; the irregularity of their arrivals and departures signaled a job that was not the traditional nine-to-five. Throughout my time in the FBI, I saw that FBI employees are generally personable, honest people with varying backgrounds; all are people who wanted to "do the right thing" in becoming FBI agents and worked hard to get there. But they are completed dedicated to their professional lives, with little left for the personal side. Out of my entire squad of eight people, only one was married with a family, besides me. Working for the FBI generally does not offer a lifestyle conducive to family life, at least not in a traditional sense. Of course, there are plenty of agents with fantastic families and wonderful children, but their families have to be flexible and make allowances for the law enforcement profession. I have heard of agents who not only missed birthday parties, but missed the actual birth of their children. By nature a reactive violent crime squad is one of the most difficult ones to combine with family life, so my experience was extreme compared to that of most FBI agents. With the varying hours required for responding to crimes and with numerous late-night or early-morning arrests, I came to long for a repetitive and structured schedule. And I came to greatly appreciate the sacrifices that agents make for our country at the expense of themselves and their families.

For the remainder of that first day, I unpacked my equipment, established my computer and email accounts, and familiarized myself with additional San Diego procedures and operations. The paperwork, phone lists, and forms were all familiar territory for someone who had previously served time in a corporate cube.

Towards the end of the day, word spread that a lead had come in regarding the location of a suspect who had robbed a bank on the previous Friday. There was the potential for an arrest that night, and all hands were needed to be on standby. I was already exhausted and felt like the day had lasted a week. I knew that Jennifer was anxiously waiting for me to hear how my first day went. I knew she would be looking forward to telling me about her first day by herself, and what she had learned about our exciting new neighborhood in Southern California. I headed home after my busy first day, but with the knowledge that I might be called to come back in to help with an arrest.

As would occur many more times during service as an FBI agent, I received a call that the FBI was proceeding with an arrest that evening, and that I needed to come back into the office and further assist with the operation. I quickly finished my meal, kissed Jennifer goodbye, and climbed back into my car and headed back to the FBI field office. What I elected not to tell Jennifer was that according to the FBI source's information, the bank robber had been jailed for serious offenses on two other occasions. In California there is a "three strikes" law that mandates a lifetime sentence for any three-time felony offender. This bank robber apparently understood the gravity of his situation, and had conveyed to the FBI source that he would not ever go back to jail and would "go down fighting." He had used a handgun in the commission of the robbery, and although he did not shoot anyone during robbery, clearly there was a significantly heightened risk of violence for this particular arrest.

As evening approached, the FBI agents met up with the San Diego Police Department in an empty parking lot a couple of miles from where the subject was believed to be located. On-site I was issued a San Diego Police Department radio, and was quickly introduced to a number of San Diego Police Department detectives and officers. They began to go over their operational procedures, and where everyone would be located for surveillance and a possible arrest. I was told to strap on my bulletproof vest and be ready for anything. I nervously strapped on my vest and was preoccupied with ensuring that my gun and handcuffs were securely fastened to my belt. I closed my trunk lid, could not locate my car keys in any of my pants pockets, and convinced myself that I had locked my keys in my trunk. I held my poker face and kept this feeling of absolute panic and terror to myself, and fortunately it turned out that the car doors were not locked and the keys were in my center console.

After allowing my pulse to slow to a somewhat normal pace, I had a surreal feeling of observing myself from an almost third-person perspective. Not only was I put into a situation in which I was working with an entirely new group of "real" FBI agents, but also "real" San Diego Police Department personnel. Up to this point my interaction with any law enforcement officers had been the result of being pulled over for speeding tickets. Not unlike most law-abiding citizens, I held a combination of fear and respect for these people, and it was hard to digest that I was now one of their peers. I had to come to terms with the fact that I was now susceptible to the same dangers as my peers, which included serious injury or death if a situation went awry. My years of following law-enforcement stories and FBI training had enlightened me on the inherent dangers of the profession, but also had taught me that the risks could be controlled and minimized. However, I was walking into one of the most risky scenarios in law-enforcement: the arrest of an armed, desperate criminal who is facing life in prison and has nothing to lose. The thought of having actual bullets flying at me, or the possibility of having to return fire, struck a primal chord. This chord would reverberate on levels deep within me until I no longer worked for the FBI.

After the group's briefing, I turned on my police and FBI radios, and took a position a few blocks from the house that was believed to be holding the subject. I listened to radio traffic and waited for several hours, which felt like days. The agents did not want the bank robber to know that we were on his trail, so the surveillance of the property involved multiple drive-bys by different agents and vehicles so that we would maintain our element of surprise. After listening to radio traffic and learning that everyone had already driven by in separate vehicles, I volunteered to take my turn and drive by the property to view the premises and see what additional intelligence I could determine. I was instructed to drive by, confirm the license plate of a vehicle in the driveway that was believed to be the subject's, and look for any movement or activity within the house. I did not know the precise location of the house, and was unfamiliar with the streets and neighborhood of this operation. I put my car into gear, rolled around the block, and then drove by the house that was described on the radio. However, I was not sure that I was even looking at the right house due to the darkness and lack of clearly visible house numbers. This was shortly before the widespread use of smartphones; I certainly could have benefitted from Google's "street view," but at the time I was using an old paper map of San Diego, which did not provide much help in this case. I thought that I saw an SUV that had been previously described as belonging to the subject, but I could not even provide 100% positive identification of that. Considering that I could not be sure that I was looking at the right house or vehicle, I certainly did not get to view the license plate or notice activity within the house. So I mustered up my most confident "FBI agent" voice and radioed back to the team that I believed I had seen the vehicle, but was unable to confirm the license plate. I did not mention that I was unsure if I had even seen the correct house. I felt uncomfortable and completely out of my element.

Shortly before midnight we finally broke off the surveillance after none of us were able to positively identify the subject. I drove home, with just enough time to grab a snack and roll into the bed. Before I feel asleep, which was difficult to do quickly because I had just experienced an intense and adrenaline-inducing event, I thought about how I would be waking up again in a few hours to unknown adventures that awaited me the next day. I had completed my first full day, which was mentally and physically draining, without any recovery time before the next day. I felt like a complete wimp for the first time in my life, and began to seriously wonder if I had made a huge mistake in joining the FBI. A part of me was already longing for my old life where I was comfortable in my tiny corporate cube doing Excel spreadsheets or process maps, and not worrying about whether I might be shot and never get to see my family again.

CHAPTER 18

First Arrest

The second day would turn out to be just as frantic as the previous one. By the end of the day I would have my first arrest statistic credited to my name. This was most definitely not because I was an outstanding agent who arrested a criminal single-handedly; no, my first and many of my future arrest stats were largely due to the generosity of my fellow agents who "shared the wealth." By crediting me with arrests, this accelerated the pace for completion of my new agent training log and served to paint a picture of an experienced and versatile squad. As with any organization, measurement and statistics are important when it comes down to budgets, funding, and performance reviews. The FBI is no different; statistics, some meaningless, are tracked and reported by agent, squad, and field office. The compiling of statistics serves multiple purposes: many agents strive to be the best agent on the best squad, in the best division. By nature, FBI agents are incredibly driven and competitive, sometimes to a fault.

After making my way downtown in the morning (which included two added detours due to my failure to take correct exits) and finding a parking spot in the mall parking garage, I strolled over to my new FBI office. Shortly after walking through the door, I was grabbed by a fellow agent on my squad, Special Agent Mark Landry. Mark asked if I would like to help him with an easy arrest that technically would occur while the prisoner was already in the state prison. In this case, a prisoner was about to be released, but had an outstanding federal prison sentence which would begin immediately after his state time was served.

As a new agent I thought this arrest would be fun, interesting, and within my comfort zone since it would be a controlled and relatively safe arrest scenario. I made sure I had my cuffs and my gun. All we needed to do was show up at the door of the state prison, handcuff our guy, and transport him to the federal prison.

Mark and I departed for the George Mason California State prison, located near the border of the United States and Mexico in a region composed of mountains and desert. After about a forty-five minute drive, we reached the prison. There was nothing else out in that area, except for a law enforcement firing range located next to the prison. This turned out to be where most of the law enforcement agencies in the San Diego vicinity, including the FBI, held their firearms training exercises. This served as a deterrent to crime, a reminder for the prisoners on the inside of what law enforcement is practicing and is capable of on the outside.

As Mark and I pulled up to the prison, I could not help but recall images from movies. Aside from a tour of Alcatraz, I had never been to a prison. *Cool Hand Luke*, *Brubaker,* and *The Shawshank Redemption* formed my impression and expectations of what a prison is like. The prison we were visiting was famous for housing celebrities such as Tom Sizemore, the talented but troubled Hollywood actor who had played a bank robber in the movie *Heat.* This film also had served as a weekend screening favorite with FBI agents at the FBI Academy. I was grateful to be going into the prison as a law-enforcement officer, rather than someone checking in for an extended and involuntary stay.

This was also my first exposure to the rigid rules and regulations of prisons. Each prison is different, but most have a policy that does not allow law enforcement officials to bring weapons into the facility. This simple rule eliminates the risk of a careless act resulting in a prisoner gaining access to a weapon.

We left our weapons locked up in the trunk of our car. Although I knew that this was an understandable and logical policy, I could not help but feel vulnerable as we walked through the door.

After waiting for about twenty minutes, we were summoned to a holding room where we could see our subject on the other side of a glass barrier. We went through a door that led us to the other side of the barrier, where we informed our subject that we were arresting him on federal human trafficking charges due to his smuggling illegal immigrants across the border into the United States. The subject was a Hispanic male in his mid-30s of average size and weight. Over time I would come to see numerous Hispanic males who were being prosecuted on this same charge. Human trafficking is done hundreds of times per day in the San Diego border region. I was getting my first taste of border-related crime. I would come to see San Diego and the surrounding border area as being the true "Wild West."

Mark allowed me to be the arresting officer. I issued my standard FBI commands for the prisoner: "Place your hands behind your back, turn around slowly, spread your legs, look to the side, and do not move!" This was it! This was my moment. I was an actual FBI agent placing handcuffs on an actual criminal. Nobody would yell, "Cut!" This was not a movie or an amusement park attraction; I was actually arresting someone.

It felt good to place handcuffs on a criminal. All of that hard work, all of the dreaming since I was young, and all of the positive choices I had made in life came down to this moment of action. The overall experience was not exactly what I originally pictured before joining the FBI; FBI agents in my mind had been the people who worked in terrorism cases or nailed Mafia families in New York. I was arresting someone on illegal alien smuggling charges, which made me feel more like a US Border Patrol agent than an FBI agent. The lines of responsibility for the FBI to work border crimes would continue to demonstrate ambiguity over the coming months; DEA, Border Patrol, local law enforcement, and the FBI all work the same type of cases:

crime that originates directly or indirectly from illegal drug and human trade between the United States and Mexico.

After completing the prison discharge paperwork, we escorted the prisoner outside to our car. I retrieved our weapons from the car trunk as Mark kept an eye on our subject. Mark was driving and knew how to get to the federal prison, so I stayed in the back seat with the prisoner, which is standard FBI protocol. We radioed the San Diego office, provided our time, mileage, and destination, and then departed the state prison. Documentation of departure time and arrival time is an important part of the standard operating procedures for the FBI, because this protocol eliminates the potential for false accusations from inmates who claim to be taken on detours and tortured. The information is recorded at the FBI office, so dates, time, and distance show the chain of custody for a prisoner and greatly reduces the potential for charges of inappropriate handling of prisoners.

We began to make our drive back to downtown San Diego to the government's Metropolitan Correctional Center, commonly referred to as MCC. Mark was an extremely effective agent but had the stereotypical dry and seemingly humorless FBI personality, at least on the surface. Mark was respectful to the prisoner, although his attitude could have easily been mistaken for a dose of sarcasm and cockiness. Mark continually asked if the temperature was okay throughout the drive. He turned on the radio and kept flipping through stations, asking our prisoner if he liked each station. However, the prisoner, who was clearly upset at having served years in the state prison only to be picked up upon his release to be taken to a federal prison, was not in the mood to be picky about the radio station he was listening to.

The prisoner was respectful towards us, which to my surprise I would find was the normal attitude directed towards FBI agents when we arrested criminals. As we drove along, I could sense his feeling of despair and of being trapped as I watched him gaze out of the rear passenger window at the streets and city landscape passing by. I knew that he knew that he had completely lost his freedom, and after years in one location was given a brief taste of driving through a city, only to be locked up for more years in another prison. I wondered what had led to his being in this situation. Over my career I would come to ponder that question many times, and I found that prisoners are not always the tough guys that I previously had imagined. Nor are they the innocent and frequently "framed" individuals that are represented in film and popular fiction. They are just people, and they are typically people who are poor and have few resources. Instead of working a minimum wage job, they want to get rich quick by participating in criminal enterprises, such as bank robberies, drug dealing, and illegal alien smuggling. Sure, there are plenty of violent and horrible criminals. But the majority of criminals are uneducated and unwilling to have a legitimate job, so they get caught doing a crime that is financially motivated. That does not necessarily make them horrible people.

This awareness was not the best attitude for me to have if I was going to continue to fight crime in the law-enforcement world. Law-enforcement officers need to be tough, they need to know that the people they are putting away are bad, and they must feel that they should not lose a wink of sleep at night because bad people got caught doing bad things. Life is simpler when everything can be neatly categorized into either black or white. But I tended to see grey; over time I was aware that I felt sympathy for some of the criminals and felt that there was zero chance that the prison system would rehabilitate them. If they went into the prison system being good people who made a bad decision, they might come out with only an education on how not to be caught the next time around. But I could not think of a better answer or magic solution to the criminal justice rehabilitation question, and besides, my job was to arrest criminals and put them in jail. My best bet would be to do so without thinking of the prisoners as people. Unfortunately, I never truly adjusted to that mode.

As we finally arrived at MCC in downtown San Diego, our prisoner was clearly getting uncomfortable. The FBI's prisoner transport policy is always to have an agent seated next to the prisoner in the back seat, with the prisoner handcuffed behind his or her back. We had previously called ahead and received an appointment time to book the subject. I learned that MCC was extremely particular about their allowable times when they would allow prisoners to be dropped off. This was not a twenty-four-hour service prison. If an agent arrested a subject late in the evening, even at seven or eight o'clock at night, he or she was out of luck; agents could not take prisoners to a federal prison after hours. We did have special arrangements with state and local jail facilities for this eventuality, but I was shocked that a large thousand-plus inmate prison facility did not have some type of intake procedures allow prisoners to be booked any time of day or night. This was the first of numerous significant process-related issues that I found myself asking about the justice system. While I had laughed at many corporate "quality improvement" initiatives, I would soon long for the days of a corporate culture of continuous improvement, because the federal government was in dire need of change.

We waited in our car to enter the prison. And we waited. And waited. After a painful hour, a person finally emerged from the loading ramp at the prison. The intake area was unmarked and looked like an area where a truck might drop off cans of soup for the prisoners. Understandably for security reasons, prisons do not want to advertise their main areas for entering and leaving the facility. I showed my credentials to the prison guard, who advised us to stow all electronics, cell phones, and weapons in the trunk of the car. This was reminiscent of my commercial airline flying experiences before I was an agent, except there were no friendly flight attendants on site. We stripped ourselves of items that were not allowed and finally escorted our prisoner into the federal prison.

This was another fascinating learning experience as an FBI agent. The federal prison reeked of a smell that I would categorize as "grungy." The environment was gritty, cold, and clammy. The staff was not at all friendly, and I could see how the years of dealing with criminals in the lower echelon of our society had taken its toll on the guards and workers; the attitude demonstrated by most prison employees mirrored the "Soup Nazi" from Seinfeld. We were whisked through a couple of different checkpoints and secure doors. We helped to stow the prisoner's possessions in bags, which he would be able to retrieve whenever he got out of prison, which was several years in the future. We signed paperwork, and the guards began to take the prisoner through the remaining steps of the intake process. A doctor had to look at each prisoner and certify that he or she was physically able to be admitted to the prison, which I discovered was far from automatic. If the prisoner was a danger to himself or others from a medical standpoint, he or she was not allowed to enter the prison and had to be taken to a local hospital where he or she would be placed under twenty-four-hour-per-day guard. This clearly was inconvenient and resource intensive for law enforcement, and I felt lucky that our prisoner was admitted with no issues.

We watched as our prisoner undressed and donned his new prison garb. We wished him good luck and were sincere with our departing words. I did not envy this young man's position.

We signed out and headed back to our car. I quickly was on the receiving end of a lecture from Mark about making small talk in front of a prisoner; Mark made it clear that he did not want the prisoners to find out where he lived. Being new to the FBI San Diego office and Mark, I had earlier asked what general vicinity of town he lived in. He quickly silenced me, which at the time I felt was ridiculous and rude. But after I learned more about the threats that agents receive from some of the most dangerous criminals in the world, I came to understand not wanting any prisoners to know what part of town I lived in, regardless of how nice they seemed.

We made it back to the office, where I began to fill out my first stack of reports and paperwork that would credit me for my first arrest. I completed my paperwork, and then wandered over to the mall food court to grab a late lunch. I thought to myself that maybe this FBI agent gig was turning out to be good after all. I was in San Diego, it was a gorgeous afternoon, and I had already arrested somebody. I was not sitting in an office or cube all day. I was out driving on the roads, seeing new scenery, and righting wrongs in the world. It really seemed like maybe I had made the right decision to enter the FBI and leave the comfortable life that I was accustomed to. I figured that for the rest of the afternoon I could continue to familiarize myself with how the San Diego office worked, and with any luck I would be heading home around five o'clock to be with Jennifer. That would be fabulous, since the previous evening's plans had been so suddenly canceled. But as the afternoon drug on, my newly assigned bank robbery pager went off and the agents in the office started scrambling. Another relatively new agent, Laura, who would prove to be a fantastic partner in my FBI endeavors, was chosen to be the case agent for this robbery. She needed help, and I needed experience, so I was drafted to serve as her partner. I cleared my schedule for the evening once again.

CHAPTER 19

First Bank Robbery

Chula Vista, California, is a community with large new subdivisions that have been built in the desert. This region has a mix of gorgeous homes along with more "colorful" areas, the kind that would cause a person to consider driving on a flat tire instead of stopping to put on a spare. Chula Vista also houses the United States Olympic Training Center, which I came to find ironic since the local feel is anything but the America that I grew up with. This area is a beehive of criminal activities ranging from drug smuggling to alien smuggling to kidnappings to bank robberies. The Mexican border proximity helps criminals by providing them a safe escape destination when eluding law enforcement officials. If a bank robber robs a bank in California, he or she only has to travel a few miles for the safety and freedom of Mexico. The Mexican government extradites only thirty to forty criminals per year; only the very worst offenders with the greatest reward for capture tend to be sent back to the United States.

After being notified of a robbery and the location of the crime, Laura and I rolled up to my first bank robbery scene. I would find that almost every day offered significant opportunities for on-the-job training. I still saw a policeman in uniform, driving a car with flashing lights and a siren, as an authority figure that I had no right to question, let alone work with as an equal or provide direction to. But in the FBI, the agents are expected to have a professional appearance, have confidence, and demonstrate leadership. The role of an FBI agent is to confidently stroll into a crime scene, quickly ascertain the situation, and in some cases take control of the investigation, which will typically involve uniformed police officers.

A dynamic that troubled me as a rookie agent was that Chula Vista had a strong police presence comprised of dedicated officers who tend to not trust others outside of their department, including the FBI. With high instances of police corruption on both sides of the border, it is understandable that the good guys only trusted those who they know with 100% certainty were also playing for the right team. Many crimes that I worked were technically both federal and state offenses, including bank robberies. So in this case, there was immediately a confrontational feeling in the air between the FBI and Chula Vista PD regarding who would ultimately drive the investigation. The Chula Vista officers numbered at least a dozen, complete with flashing lights and sirens on marked patrol cars, while the FBI had only responded with Laura and me, with less than a year of combined street experience between us.

I grabbed my notepad as I exited the car, and we briskly walked up to the entrance of the bank. I felt for my credentials inside my coat pocket several times, as if it were my weapon and as if I were walking into battle. I probably felt for that badge about as many times as an anxious skydiver who checks to make sure his or her rip-cord is present, and I was probably in a similar state of mind. I knew that this was my moment to truly play the role of an FBI agent; I wanted everyone on scene to know that I was not just a businessman visiting the bank to do business or a curious bystander. As we approached a uniformed officer who was blocking the door, we pulled out our credentials and badges and revealed the famous blue FBI letters, which showed that we were there on official federal business and belonged at the scene. The officer did not closely scrutinize our evidence of FBI employment; he made a quick and assuming nod, and we made our way into the bank.

This was my first exposure to a real robbery scene, or for that matter any crime scene of any type (with the exception of the time my brother and I became stuck in sand in our truck on a beach on Padre Island, and were informed that our truck was an "environmental crime scene"; how innocent that offense now seemed!). Laura quickly assumed control of the investigation at the scene. She spoke with the local law enforcement officers, who informed her that they were pursuing a lead at a nearby house where they believed the bank robber to be residing. There was still plenty of confusion and chaos to sort through at the bank, so we focused our efforts initially on talking to witnesses and victims at the bank, and we deferred to the Chula Vista PD . to pursue the lead about the robber's location.

Typically, FBI agents pair up for interviews of victims, witnesses, and subjects. This helps to ensure that the facts in the case are accurately recorded and understood. Ultimately one report that summarizes the interview is written, and both agents sign off on it. Fortunately, most bank robberies, including this one, are non-violent "note jobs" and are much preferable to deal with rather than crime scenes with dead victims. However, for a robbery, the victim's mental anguish and suffering cannot be understated. Over time I would interview dozens of victims who would not even be mentioned in the newspaper, but their lives were forever impacted by facing potential death in the form of looking down a robber's gun barrel. Some victims would appear calm, even after a bank robbery. Others would be visibly upset, with tears flowing. Some were in need of some professional psychological assistance, which the FBI can provide. Generally the law enforcement community considers victims to be anyone who was in the vicinity of a robbery or crime who may have had direct interaction with the criminal. Witnesses are considered to be people who saw an event happen but were not directly impacted by the criminal's actions. With most investigations, the FBI puts an immediate focus on speaking with the victims, which for bank robberies would frequently consist of only a single bank teller who gave the money to the bank robber. After interviewing anyone directly affected by the crime, investigators turn to interviewing any witnesses who may have seen the crime occur or who may have an indirect piece of information that would help solve a crime.

Helpful information from victims or witnesses usually consists of something that paints an accurate description of the subject, and often includes details such as the make and model of a getaway vehicle, unusual speech patterns, unique clothing, tattoos, sunglasses, or even the way a subject walks. These all become important individual factors in not only identifying the subject for that given robbery, but often in helping to link a criminal to multiple robberies.

For example, a subject might rob three or four banks and not get caught. Bank robbers are notorious for robbing repeatedly, since the dollar amounts they walk away with are typically less than $1,000. That amount will barely last a week in San Diego even if managed frugally, let alone if it is managed by a criminal who splurges on drugs or prostitutes. A bank robbery of over $10,000 is incredibly rare. An observant witness might comment to an investigator, for example, that a robber had a silver ring on his or her middle finger. An agent can go back and examine surveillance photos from prior robberies, and can link those together for the pictures in which the robber has a silver ring on his or her middle finger, even if completely different disguises and getaway vehicles are used. Criminals often are not smart and almost always will unknowingly reveal some minor detail that will lead to their capture. It is the job of the FBI to flush out as many details as possible and then link those together.

For the Chula Vista bank robbery that I was investigating, victims informed me that the subject had used a machete to rob the bank. He had stuck a machete down his pants, partially pulled it out, and brandished it to the teller while instructing her to give him money. Unbelievably, to make it look like he was a normal banking customer, the subject brought his expired Bank of America ATM card and placed it on the counter. In his rush to rob the bank, and with a mixture of nerves and what we suspected were powerful drugs, he managed to forget his bank card, leaving it sitting directly on the counter in front of the robbed teller. The card had his name printed in raised letters, which made for a distinctive clue and piece of evidence. I had previously heard a story about a criminal who had written a demand note on the back of a deposit slip with his name on it and left it at the scene. Here I was at my first bank robbery seeing first-hand what was possibly the dumbest bank robber in history. Figuring out who robbed the bank was going to be a slam dunk; it reminded me of how video games will commonly have an incredibly easy "tutorial mode" level to begin a game. It certainly felt like the difficulty level of my case was set to "incredibly easy."

I worked with Laura to conduct additional interviews, which were held one by one with each bank teller and with pedestrian witnesses. I was quite comfortable with this role, because I was good at talking with people and being empathetic, easily have able to put myself in other's shoes. The overall stress, pressure, and uncertainty surrounding the other aspects of the investigation were not my cup of tea, but I could interview witnesses and victims all day long without breaking a sweat. FBI agents all have their strengths and weaknesses, and I was happy to have finally found a role that I could perform well and that would add real value to the investigation.

Working my first bank robbery was quite satisfying in that I was able to see the practical application of tools that I learned at the FBI Academy, from interviewing techniques to evidence collection to the paperwork that is required to document an agent's activity in the field. But as I would continue to find throughout my time in the FBI, as soon as I began to feel some level of comfort with a task, I would suddenly find myself immersed in a new nightmare of trying to navigate a high pressure situation of critical importance. In the FBI, if an agent somehow makes an error that results in a known criminal slipping through the cracks and not being arrested, then his or her next crime is tagged unofficially as "your fault." It is not anything like working in the typical corporate world where a serious error could mean someone will not be receiving email, or worst case, a big sale could fall through. In the FBI it is up to the agents to make sure everything is done right, and one minor mistake can ultimately result in fatalities. That is a heavy burden for agents to carry.

I heard over my radio that the subject had already been arrested just a few blocks away by the Chula Vista Police Department, and that the FBI needed to arrive immediately to help with interviews, evidence collection, and next steps for the investigation. Since Laura was completely occupied at the bank, I had to travel to the arrest scene by myself. As I pulled up to the curb of an unkept house, I saw swarms of uniformed police officers, and people in handcuffs out on the lawn. My training at the FBI Academy, which had seemed never-ending at the time, suddenly felt woefully inadequate. I knew that the cops on the scene had been doing their jobs for a long time, and without a doubt held a wide array of experience with all types of criminals and arrest scenarios. And here I was, the lone FBI agent showing up, in theory with the authority to assume control of the scene, despite only having one real day of experience on the job. Once again I put on my poker face, stepped out of the car, and vowed to do my best to represent the FBI in a positive manner.

I used my people skills, which have always been one of my best assets, to the best of my ability. I was friendly and agreeable, and I deferred decisions to the CVPD Sergeant who was in charge at that scene. Sergeant David Eisenberg had the demeanor of a seasoned cop, and was sharply dressed in his uniform. I later learned that he holds a Ph.D., and is the author of an illuminating paper regarding border-related crime ("Crime, Disorder, and Public Safety in Border Communities," published through the University of Texas at El Paso). I told him that I had very recently joined the FBI, and that I was only on my second day of the job in the field. This case had both federal and state jurisdiction, and it seemed that CVPD officers were chomping at the bit to run with this case through the state criminal prosecution route. After all, they were the ones who first responded to the scene and had located and arrested the bank robber; their seemingly territorial stance was justified. I saw no reason to step on their toes or insert myself unnecessarily into their investigation.

The FBI always works as a team, including making operational decisions in working with other law enforcement agencies. I discussed the specifics of this case with Laura, who relayed that information back to our bank robbery coordinator and our squad supervisor. Due to the criminal's relatively clean history, he would not qualify for the "three strikes" California state law which puts repeat offenders behind bars for life. Therefore, it appeared that directing the case through the federal system was likely to result in a stiffer penalty for the robber. This was the direction my management passed back to us, leaving me as the messenger to an unreceptive crowd of cops who wanted to see the robber brought up on State of California charges.

Further complicating the case and adding to my discomfort was the manner in which the evidence was being gathered. The FBI has specific, rigid procedures and policies governing evidence collection. However, the CVPD had already been processing the arrest scene and gathering evidence using methods and procedures that I was unfamiliar with. I had no idea how to handle transferring evidence between separate law enforcement entities, which I knew would be tricky due to the way the chain of evidence is tracked and documented. I decided to continue to leave all evidence collection to capable CVPD, which included collection of large sums of cash that were stolen during the commission of the robbery.

I finally gathered the courage to pass along the word that the FBI was interested in pursuing federal criminal charges, and that we would need to take custody of the prisoner. In other words, "Thanks for doing all of the dirty work. Why don't you guys finish up, and we'll be taking that prisoner off your hands and chalking up a nice arrest statistic for the FBI. And you're welcome for all of the help. No really, no need to thank us." I felt ridiculous having to pass along this information, and by the face of Sergeant Eisenberg, I knew he was in no way amused or appreciative of the FBI's "help."

Laura finally joined me, and we took custody of the prisoner. We drove in to the FBI office to conduct an interview of the subject. We booked our prisoner into the FBI's system, complete with fingerprints and all identifying body marks, including piercings, tattoos, and birthmarks. This information feeds AFIS (Automated Fingerprint Information System) and NCIC (National Criminal Information Center) databases, which are nationally utilized by federal and state law enforcement.

We then began the interview and spoke with the subject for almost an hour. He broke down and cried and told us that he had committed the crime because he wanted money to try to get back together with his girlfriend, which would enable him to see the child that he had had with her. As he told us this information, I honestly believed him. Or at least, I did not doubt that he believed what he was telling us at that point. I could tell that he was sincere and sad; I genuinely felt sorry for this person. However, he had gone into a bank, was presumably drunk or high, and brandished a machete at the bank teller. He likely did not intend to harm anyone, but the mental anguish that he inflicted on those people in the bank could haunt them forever, and his actions could have resulted in someone being hurt or killed. Given his situation, he certainly had not done the right thing, which would have been getting a job and being a dedicated father for his child. But I did not see him as a truly bad person since he apparently did not intend to cause harm to others. However, the justice system does not make allowances for "nice" criminals; the reality was that he was just in the beginning stages of learning a lesson that he would have years to think about while in prison.

Our FBI office amazingly did not have a holding cell for prisoners. Our standard operating procedure was to interview prisoners while handcuffed in an interview room, and upon conclusion of the interview we were supposed to take them to the federal prison. However, San Diego's federal prison hours were severely limited, which left us in the position of having to temporarily lock up a prison in a non-federal facility overnight while waiting for a federal prison booking window. Ironically, we wound up transporting the prisoner back to Chula Vista, which was where he was originally arrested. We booked him to spend one night in the CVPD jail. Already on my second day I saw that working well with the local authorities was absolutely critical in being able to do our job successfully. And I saw that the local police often do the majority of "real" police work involved with solving crimes and arresting criminals, especially with violent crimes such as bank robberies.

The following morning, my partner and I drove to Chula Vista to pick up the prisoner. We had to get him out by a certain time, or the FBI would be charged for an extra day of "rent" to handle the prisoner; this was not unlike hotel check-out policies that I have encountered. However, our federal prison booking window was much later than our check-out time from CVPD, so we had time to kill in between. Our plan was to simply pick up the prisoner and take him back to the FBI office until it was time to head to the federal prison.

When we entered the prisoner booking area at the Chula Vista Police Department, we had to lock up our weapons in a secure area prior to entering the locked-down area of the prison facility. After locking up the weapons, we used our handcuffs and safely transitioned the prisoner from a holding cell to our car by the book. We then transported the prisoner back across the city to the FBI office. Our arrival was met with some anticipation. The majority of FBI workers are not agents, and those who are agents are typically focused on terrorism, cybercrime, or white-collar crime with more time spent at a desk than on the streets. They are as anxious as any member of the public to see a real-life bank robber. I felt proud as we pulled into the office with our bank robber in custody. I was enjoying the brief moment of being in the spotlight at the San Diego office.

The moment was short-lived. As I stepped out of the car, out of habit I instinctually felt for my gun, which an FBI agent must always keep in mind to ensure that it is secured and safe from unintended use. My face must have turned a deep shade of purple as my fingers danced around an empty holster. I plunged my fingers to the bottom of the holster, as if my gun had shrunk and I might find it if I reached far enough. I felt like Indiana Jones when he is confronted by two sword-wielding villains in the Temple of Doom and he smirks, reaches for his gun, and finds nothing but air. I thought to myself, "Wow, it is now day three and I've REALLY screwed up this time." I quietly motioned to Laura and explained her that I did not have my gun, and that I suspected that we had managed to leave our guns at the Chula Vista Police Department. Unarmed FBI agents being in charge of the custody of a bank robber is clearly not in line with the FBI's policies and procedures. I was terrified of the repercussions, but my fellow agent stayed calm and collected; she knew how to handle the situation. She would quietly get back in the car, rush back to Chula Vista, pick up our weapons, and fly back to the office. If things went smoothly, nobody would know a thing. For the third day in a row, my poker face was coming in handy.

In our fingerprinting and booking room, I sat with our prisoner by myself in an unarmed state, which was permissible since the subject was secured to a bench. The subject had no idea of our predicament, which could have been much worse if he had realized we were unarmed during our entire drive from Chula Vista back to the FBI office.

I waited for Laura to drive all the way back to CVPD to retrieve our weapons. The wait seemed like an eternity, and I was terrified that our incredibly careless error would be discovered. I even spoke with several agents who wandered down to see the prisoner, and I outwardly demonstrated my apparent boredom in having nothing to do but watch the clock, while internally I was screaming and desperate for my partner to stroll back in with weapons secured and nobody the wiser. My partner finally made it back in just over an hour, told me she could watch the prisoner and relieve me, and whispered to check her trunk as she passed me her car keys. I popped the trunk and found my beloved Glock 22 intact. I felt a wave of relief pass over me as I slipped the barrel back in the holster and secured the snap over the handle. Disaster had been averted. And a lesson had been learned, fortunately without any repercussions.

As we waited for the remainder of the afternoon, fellow squad members brought all of us burgers, fries, and shakes. They even brought food in for the prisoner. I knew this would be appreciated as something of a "last meal" since the prisoner was likely to be on a prison diet for years to come. In the FBI I always treated our prisoners with a high degree of respect and dignity, despite the crime they had committed. Aside from being the humane thing to do, it also was a potential future benefit in that an agent never knew when a prisoner's testimony or information could help the FBI down the road. If prisoners had been treated well, they were much more likely to be cooperative.

We finally escorted our prisoner to the federal prison and dropped him off, nearing my first full cycle of going to a bank robbery, performing an investigation, conducting a search, and taking a subject to jail. The only remaining part was the paperwork, which is not nearly as interesting or exciting, but consumed much more time and effort than our activities on the street. While I did not enjoy this aspect of the job, I put in my best effort at writing effectively. The importance of FBI investigative reports, which frequently are the subject of courtroom testimony and scrutiny, cannot be overstated; a well-written report can help put a criminal behind bars, and a poorly written document can result in a guilty person walking free.

CHAPTER 20

Coworkers in the Bureau

My squad mates were an interesting mix of individuals from various backgrounds. Some were former law-enforcement officers, although most were not. The agents whom I worked alongside for the most part were just normal people who had all pursued a common dream. There were a number of pranksters as well; I quickly learned never to leave my computer unattended without being password locked, and one of my squad members sent out an email to my entire squad from my account proclaiming my love for "Pookie Bear," which was intended to reflect my pet name for Jennifer, and it also proclaimed how fortunate I was to have her dress me in the morning. In some workplaces this type of prank could probably lead to an HR complaint, but FBI agents have to be thick skinned and be able to tolerate all types of behavior; I personally welcomed the spirit of trying to have some fun in a job that is frequently comprised of serious life-or-death incidents. Some of the agents were serious to a fault, but others were the kind of people who were fun to cruise around with while singing to the radio and laughing at each other's horrible vocal abilities.

My first supervisor had a background in finance prior to joining the FBI, but he loved working violent crime. Over my time spent in the San Diego office, I would have four supervisors; they all had their strengths and weaknesses, but were uniformly dedicated to the cause of fighting crime. An interesting aspect of the management structure over FBI agents is that the management comes from the ranks 100% of the time. There is no supervisor who supervises investigations and agents who did not start out as a low level agent. The only exception to this rule is the Director of the FBI, who is appointed by the president of the United States, and some of the high-level employees who are not directly over any investigative areas, such as the Chief Technology Officer, who typically come from outside the FBI due to his or her unique and specialized skill sets. But everyone who is directly involved in the management of investigations is a former agent.

The varying levels of management include supervisors who manage squads that typically range in size from a couple of agents up to twenty. Above the supervisor is the Assistant Special Agent in Charge, whom agents refer to as the ASAC. For the San Diego field office, which had approximately 250 agents, there were four ASACs. One was over all traditional criminal investigations, including my bank robbery and kidnapping squad, as well as the drug squad and alien smuggling squad. There was an ASAC for white-collar and cybercrime investigations, the area in which I felt my true talents could have been applied, but unfortunately were never taken advantage of. Another ASAC was responsible for all terrorism related investigations, both domestic and international, and finally there was an ASAC dedicated to all administrative matters, including supervision of functional areas that do not have agents, including analysts, finance, human resources, evidence handling, and photography. Interestingly, two-thirds of the FBI is comprised of these non-agent personnel. They tend to rank lower on the social totem pole, not unlike the students in a high school who are not sports stars. Despite being a gun-toting agent, I would have been happy with being a nerd behind the scenes, putting together clues to help solve crimes, but without the pressure of performing arrests, testifying, or any of the other stressful duties that accompany an agent.

The analysts and other support employees were some of the sharpest and friendliest employees in the Bureau, and often exhibited more personality than the agents that they supported. During most of my time as an agent, Kerry Hallsley supported my squad, was a hard worker, had a great deal of common sense, and kept things running behind the scenes to ensure we operated successfully, and always provided a smile and conversation that helped balance the frequently tiresome and negative nature of my squad's mission of combatting violent crime.

At the top of the management chain was the Special Agent in Charge, which was abbreviated SAC, but with the letters pronounced individually (versus calling the head honcho a "sack"). This person reported directly to the Director of the FBI. The San Diego office had three different SACs while I was stationed there. The first was clearly not a people person. During my first firearms training exercise as an agent in San Diego, I stood directly next to the SAC, whom I had not yet met. I was not positive that he was the Special Agent in Charge until I saw his name written on the paper target next to mine. I was a bit shy and did not want to disturb him, but I was hoping to have some acknowledgment or brief introduction; a "Hello," "Nice to meet you," or "Welcome to San Diego" would have been welcomed. But the SAC made no notice of my existence, which did not exactly build loyalty or respect for the leadership. I later learned that the SAC had been a football player at Notre Dame. As I stood next to him, I cranked out consistent scores of 96 and 98 (out of 100) while he struggled with scores in the 80s. Perhaps the seasoned veteran did not enjoy being schooled by the rookie, at least in this one capacity.

Before I departed the FBI, this particular SAC retired, with the rumor being that he was effectively removed from office. There was a national controversy that began on December 7, 2006, regarding the firings of several United States Attorneys around the country. United States Attorneys are appointed by the President of the United States, but traditionally only vacant positions are filled. The changing of US Attorneys midstream in the middle of the President's term is very uncommon. The

Department of Justice, ultimately directed by President George W. Bush's administration, fired seven US Attorneys around the country, which was considered by many to be politically motivated, since some of the US Attorneys had been involved with aggressively pursuing political corruption charges for some politicians, while practically ignoring similar evidence for others. What was not widely publicized in the national media was the fact that President Bush's administration had appointed most of these attorneys in the first place.

The role of United States Attorneys is incredibly powerful since they have the ability to decide which cases they will prosecute and which they will not pursue. For every crime that it is committed, few actually make it to prosecution and punishment. There are multiple phases of investigating a crime, each of which filters down the number of crimes that are able to be prosecuted. First of all, when a crime occurs, the odds are high that law enforcement will never learn about the illegal activity; many crime victims are also criminals, and they want to avoid any attention from law enforcement. Assuming a crime has occurred and the FBI is informed, the FBI looks at the evidence and proceeds with an investigation if the FBI management deems that an investigation is warranted. In many cases there will not be enough information, or there will not be a technical violation of the law, even if common sense dictates that someone is up to no good. Out of a hundred crimes that occur on the street that fall in the FBI's jurisdiction, I would estimate that fewer than five are investigated.

Ultimately, the FBI is a law enforcement agency, with the job of collecting evidence and building cases to hand over to the United States Attorney's office for prosecution. In many cases, the FBI's best efforts will not yield adequate evidence needed to prosecute a criminal, usually because the evidence simply does not exist. For example, many crimes end up being a word-of-mouth accusation which is difficult to prosecute, especially when victims are often in cahoots with the bad guys in some form or fashion. An Assistant US Attorney (AUSA) will frequently pass on pursuing a case because of lack of evidence, lack of AUSAs available to actually prosecute the case, or simply a lack of priority for the office. The US Attorney has the ability to set priorities for his or her office, which can have political impacts and ramifications. If the US Attorney in a particular district is viewed as not pursuing cases that are at the top of the agenda for the political party of the President, then he or she is in danger of being replaced, which is what happened in San Diego and elsewhere around the country. While on the surface the appearance may be that certain cases may not be pursued for political reasons, the actual reason may be due to straightforward issues that make cases virtually impossible to successfully prosecute.

Carol Lam served for a number of years successfully as the US Attorney of the Southern District of California until her abrupt dismissal by the Attorney General under the Bush administration. I have no direct knowledge or inside information regarding her dismissal, but it was not a leap to conclude that the move was strictly political and a sign of the increasing polarization between the two major political parties in the United States. Carol Lam had a stellar reputation and track record of getting results, including the successful prosecution of prominent Republican Congressman Duncan Hunter, which the FBI was heavily involved with from an investigative standpoint. Lam brought down a Republican and was fired. There may be other unknown reasons for her release. Or there may not be; the true cause and effect related to her firing remains unclear.

Lam was replaced by Karen Hewitt, who also happened to be my supervisor's sister-in-law. Much to my surprise, I was notified by an administrative area that I had been assigned as the FBI agent in charge of performing her background investigation prior to her appointment as the new US Attorney of the Southern District of California. This assignment clearly introduced a potential conflict of interest, so my supervisor stepped in and recused himself and our squad from participating in the background investigation. This type of ethical behavior was demonstrated throughout my time in the FBI, and was another example of how FBI agents try to do the right thing, even if the outcome is not always successful.

During this controversial and sensitive time for the US Department of Justice, our Special Agent in Charge replied to a media inquiry regarding his opinion on the firing of Carol Lam. He was quoted in the San Diego Times newspaper as effectively stating that he did not agree with what happened. This seemingly harmless quote that was merely an opinion proved to be more problematic than the SAC expected. The SAC reported to the Director of the FBI, who in turn reported to the Unites States Attorney General, who at the time was Alberto Gonzalez. The US Attorney General is the boss of the US Attorneys, and is the person who technically hires and fires throughout the Department of Justice; the ultimate decision making unofficially comes from the Presidential administration, who can appoint and remove the Attorney General. So in essence, our SAC was criticizing the decision of his boss's boss, and even the President to some degree. I was about to see a first-hand lesson in how politics works in a field that most people think of as being purely black and white. Apparently once an individual achieves a certain management level within the FBI, the dynamics are not unlike any other large organization where office politics results in great rewards or severe penalties, sometimes at the expense of common sense.

The San Diego FBI SAC abruptly announced his retirement and quietly left the San Diego field office in a matter of a few days. As I saw when I was next to him on the firing range, he was not a personable man, but I have no reason to doubt that overall he was a dedicated agent. While he lacked some of the leadership abilities that I would have liked to see, his resignation seemed to be forced due to his saying the wrong thing at the wrong time.

After the SAC left, the ASAC over the criminal branch, Karen Lowe, was temporarily placed in charge of the office. I held a great deal of respect for her, which was shared by all of the other agents in the office. I could not imagine the hurdles she had climbed in being a female agent in the FBI, let alone being in charge of hundreds of agents who were primarily men. She did an outstanding job during that brief tenure of responsibility for the office. She was always on-scene for important arrests, and was supportive of agents in both their professional and personal lives. The San Diego agents, including me, would have been happy to see her promoted to be the permanent SAC, but she was approaching retirement, and for family reasons did not want this position. That made me respect her even more, because in my book it showed intelligence above and beyond what can be measured by an "IQ" number; she was focusing on family and not just climbing the career ladder.

Shortly before my departure from the FBI, the SAC position in San Diego was filled by SAC Kevin Slatter, who previously had served as the assistant director of training at the FBI Academy. I was already familiar with him, since he was in charge of the FBI Academy during my stay there, and he spoke at my graduation. I had already formed a positive impression of him, because unlike many of the personalities at the Academy, he was always personable and treated everyone professionally, as a true leader should. He was also incredibly media savvy and had served as a commentator on several major networks. I knew that SAC Slatter would bring a wealth of experience to the San Diego office and would be a positive influence throughout the ranks.

CHAPTER 21

Inspections and Administration

One significant non-investigative-related experience I had was what is simply referred to in the FBI as inspection. Every three years, each field office is inspected by a dedicated team of agents from other field offices. The inspectors look at everything under the hood in a field office with a magnifying glass, including asset management, facility security, squad management, caseloads, and individual agent performance. Every single agent in the division is inspected and has a personal interview about his or her role in the FBI, including details about casework. During inspection everyone is uptight, because the entire organization is thoroughly analyzed, and the results can greatly impact the future career of everyone from agents to the SAC in a field office.

Throughout the inspection period, I was heavily utilized by multiple squads for my reporting and analysis abilities. I was effective with preparing and presenting information in an understandable and meaningful format, and I wound up having thanks from several grateful squad supervisors by the end of the inspection period. As with other occurrences, this made me question how resources, including me, were managed and utilized throughout the FBI. I felt that I added much more value doing in-depth analysis versus responding to bank robbery calls, yet during my time in the FBI I was mostly used in a role that could have been performed by anyone with a badge and gun.

As one would expect to find in any large government

bureaucracy, there were massive amounts of paperwork and procedures related to almost any action that FBI agents take short of going to the bathroom; the FBI used approximately 1,500 different forms. To some degree, that is the nature of a large organization, a necessary evil. However, at some point the amount of time agents spend on paperwork reaches a significantly diminished return in the added value. So much time is spent on paperwork, the actual work that agents were hired to do is not being done. As with many other aspects of the FBI life, the constant action that is portrayed in television and movies is far from the reality of the mundane reams of paperwork that are done back in the office.

To the credit of the organization, the FBI is not just sitting around with stacks of thousands of different types of forms saying that operations are fine and efficient. In the late 2000s, the FBI began working on the new IT project called Sentinel, which came about after a previous unsuccessful project resulted in a waste of $100 million in IT development. Sentinel was designed with a new electronic case file system, which replaced an incredibly antiquated mainframe "green screen" file system which required the maintenance of paper copies that comprise the millions of FBI files. As part of the Sentinel project, which included not only IT work but business process engineering, the number of forms used within the FBI was reduced from approximately 1500 down to 200. Business process improvement efficiencies were being looked at, and repetitive or redundant forms were condensed or consolidated where possible. The success of this endeavor was critical in enabling agents to spend more time investigating and less time with managing administrative overhead tasks. The project was finally completed in 2012.

I estimate that there are about eight hours of indirect work such as filling out paperwork, filling up with a tank of gas, or visiting a judge or attorney, to one hour of direct investigative work. The administrative work of preparing court documents, writing records, briefing supervisors, and other necessary indirect actions that go with the job sometimes seemed to be the only tasks we were able to work on, which did not contribute to improved job satisfaction for agents.

When performing an investigation, not only does the agent have to think about the time that needs to be dedicated to the activity, but also the appropriate permissions that are mandated by FBI policy that must be obtained before proceeding with most investigative activities. When figuring out a game plan for an investigation and the methods to be used, agents have to factor in the amount of administrative time needed, and many times the more advanced investigative techniques are not worth the amount of time that it will take just on the administrative side. Sometimes what would be a useful investigative technique will be avoided because the agent just does not have time to fill out reams of paperwork after the fact.

For example, various forms of telephone monitoring can yield fantastic investigative results. However, the federal government, the citizens who make up the United States, and FBI agents are all extremely sensitive to privacy issues, and rightfully so. If somebody has conversations that an agent wishes to monitor, a strict set of protocols, including proof that monitoring is necessary, must be followed prior to the actual monitoring. This protection of our freedom comes at a cost. If somebody has been kidnapped, the FBI is given the difficult task of trying to locate this person. If safety is an issue, the FBI has a mechanism to monitor a cell phone's geographic location, but is restricted to only obtaining that information. Telephone calls or the content of those calls is still forbidden without a court order. Just to apply for a court order requires various approvals within the FBI, including supervisors and the Assistant Special Agent in Charge. In addition, an agent must fill out several pages of paperwork which supports and justifies the requested court order. Next, the United States Attorney's office has to prepare additional court documents. After this is completed, the FBI agent has to go and meet with a judge and swear to the facts in order to proceed with the court order and get the electronic monitoring up and running. Finally, once the court order is signed and filed, it must be provided to the appropriate telephone company, who then will make the necessary technical arrangements for the FBI to begin monitoring. At this point, even working at a frantic pace, a day may have passed for all of the pieces to align, and with a kidnapping, that is by far the most critical day in the process. In order to preserve our freedom, the cost is not only monetary when looking at the number of resources and administrative time associated with telephone monitoring, but it is also literally a cost of lives lost who could have been saved if broader and more flexible monitoring policies were allowed by the FBI. It is easy to sit in a classroom or online comment section and preach about how we need to further protect our liberties. Who can argue with that? Well, anyone with a kidnapped loved one who has to endure waiting for news is going to be incredibly unhappy with the current system and process that indeed protects our liberties and privacy. Unfortunately, during the course of investigating more than fifty kidnappings, never once did other squad members or I successfully establish telephone monitoring. It was not that we did not want to do that, but it was not practical due to the time and administrative investment required.

People often think that the FBI is listening to their phone calls. Most people have no idea how incredibly rare a "phone tap" is, largely due to the previously described processes that must be navigated through. I listened in and monitored telephone conversations for only two cases throughout my time in San Diego. To my knowledge, those were the only two active cases in the San Diego area during that time with telephone monitoring. Not millions, thousands, or even dozens of cases. Two. Except when safety is an issue, telephone conversations can only be monitored for criminal matters when all other investigative techniques have been exhausted. Agents have to demonstrate that interviews, surveillance, and undercover employees cannot provide the necessary information for an investigation; telephone monitoring is the last resort.

The phone conversations that I listed to were related to organized crime cases with multiple subjects and a variety of cellular telephone lines that required monitoring. Before listening in on a phone conversation, the FBI must go through what is called a minimization procedure. An Assistant United States Attorney will go over with the FBI agents what they are and are not allowed to monitor. Phones can only be monitored for content that is relevant to the investigation, which is the same concept used for search warrants. When performing a physical search, the agent can only search in the locations that are allowed, areas that could possibly store or conceal the items that pertain to the investigation. With a monitored phone call, only the parts of the phone call that pertain to an investigation can be listened to.

So how on earth can an FBI agent possibly get the evidence he or she needs for an investigation by listening to only parts of a phone conversation? The FBI can only listen for brief segments and make a judgment on whether the content is relevant. If the content is not relevant (such as a criminal's spouse who is talking about recipes with a friend), then the agent stops listening for approximately 30 seconds. Then the agent will listen in again for a few seconds, and once again will try to tell if the conversation has gone a direction that allows monitoring. If not, they must immediately stop listening and will keep repeating the same 30 second cycle for the duration of the phone call. Although some criminals are not aware of this protocol, many of the more savvy subjects, especially law breakers with ties to organized crime, actually use their children to talk to other children to pass along information since they know FBI agents will not be allowed to listen to their children speaking. The perception of FBI agents being able to pick up a phone or just tap into the phone whenever they want to listen is greatly exaggerated in the imagination of the public, which in the long run only helps criminals and terrorists.

There are two scenarios in which the normal rules of

telephone monitoring do not apply. One is related to the monitoring of telephone conversations that occur in prisons. Prisoners give up all rights related to searches, and written correspondence and telephone conversations are considered to be part of the search rights that are given up. When a prisoner makes a call, or even uses the closed-circuit audio system with telephone handsets to speak with visitors, those conversations are typically automatically electronically recorded. The vast majority of this content is never listened to, but in some cases agents will obtain recordings. Once again, to do this there are significant administrative requirements along with a cumbersome process that involves working with the United States Attorney's office, but a formal court order is not necessary.

The other scenario that allows telephone monitoring is for special circumstances regarding terrorism investigations. The FBI has obviously concentrated efforts on combating terrorism in the post 9/11 world. This is the area where controversy has arisen around what are called national security letters. A national security letter is a mechanism that an agent can use to get telephone information, such as a listing of incoming and outgoing call details. Terrorism agents and analysts work tirelessly in trying to put together bits and pieces of information and see how they relate. Certain intersections of information can prove to be fruitful and truly prevent devastating attacks. The national security letter serves as a documentation and justification requirement to authorize telephone related activities. FBI agents are busy people, with numerous leads to investigate, and do not have spare time on their hands. FBI agents do not care about getting telephone information unless it is pertinent to one of their investigations. They are human and want to do the right thing. However, if an investigative lead goes nowhere, they may be tempted to move on to the next investigative step, and sometimes may not appropriately follow-up with the correct administrative steps for dead-end leads. When this breakdown in the administrative process pertaining to national security letters became apparent, it resulted in a significant negative media coverage and related inquiries about FBI agents, who the public was lead to believe were just monitoring phones with blatant recklessness and zero regard for privacy. Citizens imagined rooms full of FBI agents spying on their telephone conversations. The reality is that this monitoring did not consist of actually listening to telephone conversations, which requires additional levels of approval and documentation as allowed by FISA (Foreign Intelligence Surveillance Act). These abuses have been greatly exaggerated; FBI agents are some of the staunchest believers in the Constitution and the privacy and protection afforded to all citizens. Surely, there was some sloppiness in documenting the appropriate National Security Letters, but the public perception of FBI agent telephone spying abuse was incredibly far from the reality of a few documents that were not appropriately submitted.

In 2013 there was an AP article published on how Google was forced to hand over user information to the FBI, which was legally authorized through National Security Letters. The first comment that I noticed when viewed on Yahoo plainly stated, "The FBI is the enemy." There were seventy thumbs-up votes from people who agreed. There were zero thumbs-down until I voted. Clearly the FBI has overwhelming trust and image problems that are amplified by social media outlets. I was saddened to realize that our own citizens are so poorly educated on how the dedicated, highly principled people of the FBI are giving their lives to protect the country; the United States has plenty of enemies, but the FBI is most certainly not one of them.

CHAPTER 22

Background Checks

A significant part of my time in San Diego was spent working on background investigations. New agents are expected to perform background checks, which agents consider to be a fairly mundane and routine process. These investigations are primarily related to appointments or positions appointed by the President of the United States. In addition, there were investigations related to Presidential pardons.

Background checks are centrally managed from Washington, DC, but the actual ground-work is done in the field offices. The work is initiated by what the FBI calls a lead. A lead is the FBI's formal mechanism communicating from one field office to another that action is required pertaining to an investigation. Rather than an agent picking up the phone, this method puts requests in writing and has a system whereby information can be exchanged and returned. In addition, this method helps field offices manage due dates and priorities. The same mechanism is used for all types of investigations, from background checks to bank robberies. For example, if a bank robber robs a bank in San Diego and then the FBI learns that the subject may have fled to Phoenix, the San Diego office would enter a high-priority lead for the Phoenix office to follow up to try to locate the robber. My squad in San Diego covered leads for all of the major types of violations that we worked, including bank robberies, kidnappings, extortions, fugitives, murder-for-hire schemes, and crimes against federal officials. In addition to these, along with all squads, new agents were tasked with working leads pertaining to background checks.

While background check leads were assigned to new agents because the seasoned agents viewed this as boring and tedious busywork, I personally found these missions to be an enjoyable, relaxing way to get out of the office. I thoroughly enjoyed talking to people and getting to play the role of FBI agent without the danger of going after the bad guys that I was accustomed to. I loved having a break from the pressure and stress of my normal violent crime assignments.

Interviews conducted during an FBI background check follow a specific script that helps determine eight characteristics to form an overall representation of an individual's character. These same questions are used regardless of the subject of the background investigation; potential FBI agents, US Attorney appointees, and convicts who are hoping to get a pardon all go through the same set of questions. I cannot disclose what the questions or characteristics are, but they cover a broad spectrum of personality traits and provide a standardized common-sense approach. Unfortunately, agents are not allowed to determine their own questions, and during an interview there could be additional areas that an agent would be interested in, but the FBI strictly follows a defined script and sticks only to allowing the prescribed set of questions. This was disappointing to me, and seemed to take away from the ability of agents to perform their job and really try to flush out problems or issues that the standard questions might not address. There is a balance between ensuring standardization and efficiency versus the quality of the product. To use a food analogy, the FBI tends to take the "McDonalds" approach, while I would have preferred to be able to customize my burger based on the individual "customers." This tactic felt more like the process that a military branch would follow. Across numerous areas, a military influence can be seen in the FBI. For the most part this structure is good and understandable, but it is not always desirable.

My first background check was for a man who was asking for a Presidential pardon. My specific assignment was to interview friends and coworkers of this individual in the San

Diego area to get information that would allow the government to effectively determine if he had changed his ways for the better. For this assignment I teamed up with my partner, Special Agent Woodrow, and we set out to interview several people who had knowledge of the person who was seeking the pardon. This person had already served his prison sentence and had been out of prison for nearly two decades. He wanted to be able to return to a fully normal life. At least on paper, he made a strong argument to support his request. In the 1980s, this man owned a television and satellite business and was selling satellite boxes that had been modified to receive any channel (including premium channels such as HBO) without paying anything extra. That was the technology rage at the time, and even as a young and relatively young teenager in the 80s, I remember seeing numerous magazine advertisements for cable boxes and descramblers that would allow people to watch all satellite television stations for "free." This man sold several hundred illegally modified satellite boxes through his business before he was shut down by federal authorities. He wound up serving several years in federal prison for his crime. He was a businessman and had never been a violent criminal. Clearly, he had gone along with a "sheep" mentality and assumed that since thousands of businesses were openly doing the same thing, he would not be caught or punished. This is not a far stretch from the pack mentality of speeding along at the same rate as everyone else, regardless of whether a driver is technically over the speed limit (and by the way, FBI agents, including me, speed every single day).

After his arrest and after serving prison time, the man acknowledged that what he had done was absolutely wrong. Since being released from prison, he had gone on to be a contributing member of the community, had obtained his real estate license, and was generally successful. However, being a felon had continued to cause problems; for example, when he wanted to coach his son's soccer team, the question of whether he had been convicted of a felony was asked on the application, and he did not lie and was therefore banned from being able to coach. In general, people should treat felons with special caution. Felons tend to be repeat criminals, and they have deservedly put themselves in a position of distrust. However, this man had a spotless record prior to his offense, and had been out of jail for seventeen years without a single blip on his record. Seeing that he had gone on to marry, to have a family, to hold down steady jobs, and to provide a stable household for his children, I personally thought he seemed like an appropriate person to receive a Presidential pardon. In fact, all things considered, he seemed to have greater character than most non-felons that I have met.

We went to interview various people who had knowledge of this man and came across a number of interesting characters throughout the process. One was a wealthy doctor who lived on top of a hill with a beautiful house in the San Diego area. Unfortunately, he was a lonely man; his wife had recently passed away. He was older, a bit eccentric, and was happy to have our company. Other friends and associates that we visited were obviously impressed with our status as FBI agents and treated us like royalty. It was fun knocking on the doors of people who were not expecting a visit from anyone, and then displaying FBI credentials and introducing ourselves. Most members of the public never meet an FBI agent (that they are aware of, anyway), and once they recover from the surprise of meeting one, they are curious and have more questions than a first grader. I always enjoyed the part of the job involving showing people that FBI agents are just regular people, and are usually nothing like the bland personality that is represented by the stereotypical agent.

One person whom we visited as part of a background investigation insisted on sending us away with a sack full of fresh avocados. These were freshly picked from a tree in his yard. The FBI is careful not to accept favors or gifts. FBI agents are allowed to receive items up to twenty dollars of value, and are strongly encouraged not to even accept any gifts of any type of any value whatsoever. But this man insisted that he had so many avocados that they would start going bad, and I could tell that it would make a nice story for him to say he not only met some FBI agents, but he sent the agents home with avocados. So I accepted his offer, which clearly lit up his face with a huge grin, and later Jennifer and I shared our own grins while enjoying the best avocados I have ever tasted.

Background investigations that I worked on included federal judges and other high-level government officials. Most people that contributed to the investigations were eager to share information and were proud to be participating in part of the background check process, even if they only played a small role. People that do not have anything to fear or hide generally love working with the FBI, and no doubt enjoy having a glimpse of how the most elite law enforcement agency in the world operates. Frequently these interviews are performed by semi-retired agents beyond the age of fifty-seven who still wish to be involved with the FBI on a temporary contract basis. These older agents retain their credentials and present themselves as FBI agents, and still enjoy working with the public and sharing an occasional war story about their careers. These resources are valuable not only because of their experience and judgment, but also because they free up resources within the FBI who are focused on higher priority items.

Unfortunately, my time spent on background investigations would only be a small percentage of my work time in the FBI. However, despite the bland reputation that this duty had, it proved to be one of the most enjoyable activities I performed as an agent.

CHAPTER 23

Off Duty

I thoroughly enjoyed being an FBI agent when I was not working. It was fun to go to a movie and see FBI agents on the big screen, knowing that if the person sitting next to me realized they were sitting next to an actual agent, they would likely be quite shocked. While seeing the movie *Breach*, I looked around the theater and counted six other FBI agents that I recognized. Little did the crowd know that they were surrounded by FBI agents while watching this movie about FBI agents!

Shortly after arriving in San Diego, Jennifer and I decided to eat at a local diner in the Mission Valley area. Towards the end of the meal, I realized that I did not have enough cash to pay for the meal and would need to pay with a credit card. I did not yet have my California driver's license, and I had managed to misplace my Texas license when we moved. My only photo identification was my FBI credentials. FBI agents are not supposed to use their credentials unless it is for FBI business, but I did not have an alternative; I concluded that eating is an essential function for an FBI agent so therefore I would be justified in using my credentials. And quite frankly, as a new agent I was proud and wanted to show off the fact that I was an FBI agent.

When I produced my credentials and showed my picture with the big blue FBI letters in the background, the waitress chuckled and said that it was a decent fake of real FBI identification. She went on to verbally compare my credentials to a fake Elvis driver's license she had once seen. I laughed and told her that the ID was authentic, and that I had no alternative form of photo identification. She still did not believe me and became visibly flustered. In her mind, I might as well of had the Elvis driver's license and then seriously told her that I was Elvis. I explained to her that it would be a felony for someone to masquerade as an FBI agent with credentials, and that as an FBI agent, I enforced federal law and would be the last person on earth to attempt to use a fake identification, which would be breaking the very laws that I was responsible for upholding. I also offered that she could call the San Diego FBI field office and ask to speak with my supervisor. Thank goodness, she did not take me up on this, because this probably would have resulted in a less than positive impression by my new boss. Supervisors are under intense pressure and have real problems to deal with. An agent inappropriately identifying himself as an FBI agent so he or she can complete a financial transaction at a diner does not qualify as a real problem. Fortunately, the waitress finally accepted the credit card and processed it for payment, but I do not believe she ever thought that the credentials were real. If only airport workers and others who are in a position where this type of identification should be scrutinized would take their job as seriously as this waitress, the country would probably be a much safer place.

FBI agents who are off-duty never know when they may be needed if there are no other law enforcement officers around. That ultimately proves to be a burden for FBI agents. Agents are not just members of the public; they are expected to uphold the laws of the state where they are located, and if presented with a life-threatening situation or scenario, even if it does not violate federal law and there are no police officers present, FBI agents have a duty to act.

On one gorgeous San Diego sunny Saturday afternoon, Jennifer and I stopped by a local strip mall in our Tierrasanta neighborhood to eat burritos for lunch. She pointed out a group of people who were clustered outside of a pizza restaurant that was located in the same strip center complex. It was apparent that there was a heated argument in progress. It is certainly not an FBI agent's duty to resolve arguments in a public place; that is up to private citizens to do on their own time. However, in this situation there was an adult male in his 30s, a younger teenager, and several other individuals who were participating in this argument. There was yelling, and the situation obviously had a high potential to escalate to physical violence. The teenager, who was dressed in a baseball uniform, seemed to be arguing with a man who appeared to be his coach. The other two individuals appeared to be the kid's parents, and the coach was yelling at the boy and his mother. The father who was standing by had a bewildered look as though he did not know what to do and wished he could be anywhere else on the planet. I had no doubt that the father was caught in a dilemma of knowing that he and his family should walk away from the argument, but that he also should be expected to stand by his family, even if the confrontation turned from verbal to physical.

I happened to be wearing flip-flop sandals, shorts, and a t-shirt with a gigantic Piggly Wiggly grocery store mascot on the front. Luckily, I also had my credentials and badge with me, although I did not have my weapon or handcuffs. Armed with only my experience and badge, I simply walked right up to this angry crowd, announced my position as a law enforcement officer with the FBI, and explained that if things escalated, there quickly could be assault charges filed for all involved parties. I encouraged the participants of the argument to step back, think about what they were doing, and see that it was a nice day on which they should just walk away from this situation. I physically inserted myself between the coach and the high school kid, and they did back down, although they were still red in the face and had their chests puffed out like two angry roosters, not wanting to appear to be relenting to the other party. The father was extremely appreciative and repeatedly said, "Thank you, sir," and I could tell that he was relieved that the dispute had been resolved safely and that nobody was going to be injured or in trouble with the law. His wife still had a vicious look on her face, but all parties knew that I was serious, based on the authority in my actions and voice. While inserting me into the situation may not have been the safest move on my part, I did feel, based on my judgment, that it was the right thing to do. Although I did not have a weapon, at a glance I could safely assume that these people were not armed drug dealers and would probably respond predictably to an authority figure with the power to arrest them and get them into a mountain of legal trouble. After the parties dispersed, Jennifer and I returned to our original mission of eating lunch. As I sat down to eat my burrito, I felt a sense of pride knowing that I had taken the correct course of action.

On another occasion, Jennifer and I were enjoying the fresh ocean air on a pier at Ocean Beach. California beaches are legally designated as non-smoking areas, in addition to surrounding piers and walkways. Sure enough, we encountered a group of teens who looked like possible gang members smoking on the pier. Smoking is the reason my father died before the age of sixty. While I think people have the right to smoke in their own homes, people who do not smoke have the right not to be impacted by smokers. I nicely asked the teens to stop smoking and pointed out that it is illegal for them to do so. They gave me a dirty look and continued smoking. I then pulled out my badge and credentials. Without explaining that I was an FBI agent, but with an obvious display that I was in law enforcement, I ordered them to immediately put out their cigarettes because they were violating the law. They still did not look happy, but they did comply with my order. If they had continued to smoke, realistically, I would not have tried to do anything because I would have been outnumbered and would have escalated the situation unnecessarily. But in this case my display of authority worked, and it felt good to have that power to right a minor wrong. At that moment, my status as an FBI agent was a blessing that I was thankful for.

Another area of responsibility that just a few years prior I could not have imagined was flying armed in a post 9/11 world. At the FBI Academy, as part of the firearms instruction, new agent trainees learn basic tactics to use on an airplane if confronted with a violent situation, such as the events that occurred on September 11, 2001. There are few responsibilities that are greater than flying armed and being directly responsible for addressing threats while on an airplane with hundreds of other passengers. On several occasions, on flights for both work and pleasure, I flew as an armed FBI agent and was effectively a sky marshal on those flights. On most flights I was the only person flying armed, so I knew that if things went awry, I would be the only person on the plane with responsibility to do what was necessary to neutralize a threat. A worst case situation could mean having to bring down a plane so that a crowded stadium or other target could be spared, much like what the people on board the flight in Pennsylvania did on United Flight 93 on September 11, 2001. It is difficult to relax and enjoy a flight with the knowledge that in any given second, terrorists could run up and down the aisles, slashing the throats of people whom they deem as barriers to their taking over the plane. But this is what happened on 9/11, and therefore there is a real possibility that it could happen again.

On some flights I was ushered into the plane early and greeted by the captain. In those cases I showed my credentials and introduced myself, and allowed the captain to decide if he or she was comfortable with the fact that I would be flying armed. Pilots are the captains of their ships and have the right not to allow agents to fly armed on their airplanes. In that case, an armed FBI agent would have to take a different flight. That experience never happened to me, and most pilots were friendly and seemed grateful to have the extra protection on the airplane. There were some flights that had other armed personnel, and we all knew each other's locations on the plane in case of emergency. Fortunately nothing threatening ever did happen on those flights, but I will never forget the feeling of having a gun on the plane, eyeing people that looked suspicious, and continually formulating my strategy to take action if something bad occurred. While life outside of work for an FBI agent is enjoyable, there really is no such thing as true "free time" for an FBI agent; FBI agents must be ready to act twenty-four hours per day, seven days per week.

CHAPTER 24

Baker to Vegas

Within the law enforcement community, there is an annual team footrace that attracts hundreds of participating law enforcement organizations represented by thousands of individual participants. This event, known as Baker to Vegas, is the largest competitive running event held for law enforcement in the world. The majority of the teams are from the southwestern United States, but teams from all over the United States and even international teams fly in for the competition. The course winds from Baker, California, to Las Vegas, Nevada, over 120 miles of desolate desert and mountain roads. Teams are comprised of twenty members who split up the course by running relay legs ranging from five to ten miles each.

The San Diego FBI fields a team for this event each year. While the race is held with a fun spirit of camaraderie among law enforcement agencies, there is no question about the level of commitment and competition that is displayed. Law enforcement tends to attract competitive individuals, and the Baker to Vegas event highlights this common DNA found throughout the law enforcement community. Competition within the San Diego office was stiff to make the team. While I was not in the greatest shape of my life, my natural running abilities propelled me to finishing strong enough in a time trial to secure a spot on the team. I could hardly wait to participate in this event.

I was assigned to run a seven-mile leg in the relay. I studied the course elevation, and calculated that I would be running in the mountains in the middle of the night. I prepared for several months in advance with a training regimen that included plenty of hills. Unfortunately, to this day, my knees are not thankful for the abuse that I put them through; bending my legs sounds like I have bags of marbles hidden under my knee caps. But it was worth it.

The team members spanned agents from a variety of squads in San Diego, with mostly male but a few female racers. This was a fit bunch of people, but fit was not a term that I would use to describe many of the agents in the office. A number were overweight, and I was amazed that some could ever have been in shape to pass the physical exam to get into the FBI. Fortunately for them, the FBI does not have ongoing physical tests for agents; only firearms proficiency is tested periodically once an agent graduates from the FBI Academy.

The weekend of the race finally arrived. Jennifer and I booked a hotel in Las Vegas and then rode with other agents to the race course. I was in awe of the incredible amount of logistics that were involved. With multiple vehicles and runners on the roadway, I was surprised that injuries or accidents were not common. However, the participants were all active law enforcement members, so they were capable of operating safely in these challenging conditions. If a similar event were open to the public, the results would have been disastrous.

The hundreds of teams that participated in the race were organized into competitive groupings based on size. We were in an extremely competitive division composed of about 30 teams. The entire team treated the event as if winning would provide world peace. I treated my leg of the race accordingly, and put more effort into that race than I had ever put into any other physical endeavor.

Waiting for my leg of the race to start seemed like an eternity. When I finally took the baton, my team was in a respectable second place. Ahead by about a quarter mile was the San Diego DEA team. While we were frequent partners in law enforcement operations, we were bitter rivals in this race. I vowed to run down the DEA agent by the end of my relay leg. He was thin and athletic, and clearly weighed less than I did by at least thirty pounds. But I knew that despite being heavier, I was a natural runner and that I could endure the pain that comes with running fast better than most.

As I raced through the cool night desert air, complete with a black sky peppered by thousands of shining stars, I felt incredibly alive. I was soaring down the road, experienced moments of elation when I thought to myself, "Wow, I am running a race as an agent on the FBI team!" I slowly caught up to the DEA agent, put on a kick that Olympians would be proud of, and passed him like he was standing still. A few hundred yards later, I backed off the pace. I gasped and was feeling the pain of my anaerobic efforts, but I was thrilled to have put my team in the lead. I finished up my leg and pushed as hard as I could to the baton relay point. I collapsed by the road, felt sick, and looked like hell, but I was beaming.

The race continued on through the night. I learned that at some point the DEA had an incredibly fast runner who reclaimed the lead, and they were able to finish ahead of us. But we still finished up second in our division, which was a great accomplishment. I have won countless trophies, ribbons, and medals for road races, including overall wins, but my second place Baker-to-Vegas award mug is my most prized possession for running. While I was not in love with my career in the FBI per se, the camaraderie and experiences that I shared with other agents was priceless.

CHAPTER 25

Face of the FBI

The FBI rotates the duty of answering incoming calls and visitors among agents so that no one agent is permanently stuck performing this desk job which is referred to as "the duty agent." Answering phones and being the public face of the FBI sometimes could be stressful but also proved to be entertaining and sometimes comical. On numerous occasions, I was the first "real" FBI agent that a person had ever met. I tried my best to assume the intelligent and professional image that I assumed people had in their mind of what an FBI agent is like. However, many of the citizens who strolled through the doors of the FBI were most certainly not what I had envisioned as "normal" people who need help from the FBI. Most of the crimes reported to the FBI are serious, but like moths to a flame, the FBI tends to attract more than their fair share of lunatics.

While I was the duty agent, people shared several ludicrous stories with me. One person thought the government was spying on him, but since he was convinced it was the CIA, he though the FBI could assist; in his mind the FBI and CIA were rivals, and he wanted "Team FBI's" help. Another person visited the office and reported that he had been kidnapped, and that while he was kidnapped, the government had placed radio implants in his head; he truly believed that his every thought was being read by the government. He seemed genuinely surprised that I was not aware of this already, since clearly I worked for the government and must have access to the radio transmissions that were "beaming" out his every thought.

On these occasions I eventually would have to stop the person from talking (which was usually a difficult task), and then tell him or her that I believed that he or she was trying to be honest, but that unfortunately I could not help him or her. I then would recommend to the person that he or she seek professional help for mental illness. I had been around unstable people before, but to be put in a position in which I had to tell someone that he or she was mentally ill made for quite an unpleasant conversation. Directly accusing people of being mentally ill would infuriate them, because they truly believed what they were saying were true. I always was professional and told these people that if they could produce evidence that would substantiate that what they were saying were true, then we would certainly take their claims seriously.

Sometimes people would refuse to leave the FBI property. They would continue to talk indefinitely and would spin increasingly outrageous stories. I was always prepared for a physical attack, because people that demonstrate this type of extreme instability or delusions can be incredibly unpredictable and dangerous. For such an event, we would call in the FBI security guards, who were uniformed and armed, and we would have to have some people physically removed from the FBI grounds. When that occurred, the person's name and information would be added to our 5150 file, which was a repository of mentally unstable people who were no longer allowed on FBI grounds. 5150 is the section number in the California legal code that authorizes the involuntary handling of mentally unstable people who pose a threat of danger to themselves or others. We simply referred to people that were in the file as 5150s. I frequently see popular culture references to 5150s, and that term will always have a special meaning for me since I had to deal with some of the actual delusional people in the world that make up real 5150 files.

Part III

Never a Dull Moment

CHAPTER 26

Early Bird

My first major planned arrest, as opposed to reactive arrests for bank robbers which typically are not planned out in advance, was for a subject facing charges for alien smuggling. This woman was the girlfriend of a corrupt customs agent, who also was facing arrest; the customs agent was known to accept cash bribes to allow vehicles to pass into the United States without being inspected. Obviously allowing vehicles that are ferrying some type of illegal objects or people into the United States is a huge problem. Not only does this contribute to illegal immigration, but allows illegal drugs into the country, and can even be a mechanism that enables foreign terrorists to set foot on American soil.

There were several other arrest locations and sites that were part of a large coordinated effort. This was my first experience with an organized full-scale arrest scenario, and reminded me of what I had seen in movies in which the entire operation involved multiple agencies, including FBI, U.S. Customs and Border Patrol, and Immigration and Customs Enforcement, also known as ICE. The arrest plan, which was a standard document prepared prior to each planned FBI arrest, called for what was known as "knock and announce." That means that at 6:00 a.m., agents planned to knock on the door and yell for the occupants to open up; and after a few seconds the door would be broken in if there was no response. To have all of the pieces in place, this meant getting up by 4:00 a.m., meeting and assembling by 5:00 a.m., with the arrest occurring at 6:00 a.m., an hour which has legally been upheld as a reasonable time to perform searches and arrests. Arrests late in the evening or earlier in the morning require documentation of special circumstances and a special court order, which is not easily obtained.

As part of determining an arrest plan, we had to locate and document the nearest high-level trauma hospital in case of someone, either a suspect or an agent, being shot. The FBI likes to plan for every conceivable scenario so that things go as smoothly and safely as possible. Also pre-planned is the role that each person is assigned to play during the arrest. Since I was a new agent, I did not expect to play a significant role during the arrest; I expected to provide backup, crowd control, and possibly a few minor supporting roles. However, since I was the largest person out of all the agents in my arrest team, and after getting suggestive glances when the arrest team leader asked for a volunteer to take the battering ram and be the lead when approaching the house, somehow I found myself raising my hand and mumbling, "I'll do it." I had seen this on TV hundreds of times, and with my training I knew that this is the most dangerous position on an arrest team. But I was anxious to establish my reputation as a good agent; I needed to get experience doing everything, and that included performing dangerous roles under pressure. Besides, I clearly was the largest person and the most logical candidate for the job. As we approached 6:00 a.m., images kept flashing through my head of my having to break the door down and finding myself standing in the doorway, also known as the "fatal funnel," armed only with a fifty-pound battering ram and no gun. I could envision a team of drug cartel members just waiting for me to break the door open before pulling their triggers to unload packed magazines from automatic weapons. I knew this was a risk, but I reasoned that if I hustled and immediately got out of harm's way, even if there was gunfire, I had a good chance of not being hit. Still, knowing that there was any elevated risk of being shot tended to get my adrenaline flowing.

The agents drove from our pre-arrest assembly point to the

site of the arrest in several unmarked cars. We did not want to announce our presence, so we ran without lights or a siren. Despite this, any early-morning dog walkers would have immediately noticed the site of multiple dark window tinted sedans screaming through a neighborhood at about 60 mph. We just hoped we would not attract the attention of the occupants of our arrest location.

It was incredibly exciting to roll up to the house, knowing what we planned to do, and yet not knowing what would actually happen. I grasped my battering ram, checked my bulletproof vest straps, and felt for my sidearm location in the event that I would need to discard the battering ram and draw my weapon as fast as possible. Our cars parked a few houses down the street from the target house, and agents poured from car doors and immediately assembled in a line, just as my training had prepared me for. I was the second person in the line of agents. The battering ram, which earlier felt heavy, now felt as light as a feather. My body was on fully-automatic mode at that point, with my heart pounding like crazy as we approached the front door. The agent in charge of the arrest led the group to the door, with everyone lined up and visually scanning doors and windows for movement. I felt extremely vulnerable as the agent pounded on the door yelling, "FBI, we have a warrant, open up the door immediately!!"

From personal experience, I believed that the majority of people were still fast asleep at 6:00 a.m., especially criminals who are not exactly known for being hard-working early risers. If someone knocked on my front door at that time of day, it would probably take me at least a full minute to get some clothes on, and then I would try to figure out who was there, what they wanted, and whether they posed a threat. But for this arrest, after a few seconds went by, my logic and reasoning took an imaginative turn, and suddenly I envisioning tattooed gangsters and criminals pulling out their weapons, popping clips into their automatic machine guns, and aiming for the door. A few more seconds went by and the agent pounded on the door again, but nobody opened up. My heart rate must have been approaching 200 at that point; the adrenaline was flowing and I had reached a primal fight or flight mode. The lead agent looked back at me and nodded, meaning that it was my turn to step up and knock in the door using the battering ram.

In an instant as I was stepping into position, the door opened up and a teenage girl's face appeared. The battering ram would not have to be used on that day. I jumped out of the doorway, set the ram down, pulled out my weapon, and felt comforted that my own life was mostly now back in my own hands, and that it appeared that the subjects and other residents of the house would fully comply with the arrest team.

We got to work and followed our standard operating procedures for that situation, which entailed removing the girl from the scene. According to the girl, her mother, who was the target of this arrest, was not home. Agents can always count on criminals lying on behalf of their family members, but my instincts told me that this sleepy teenager truly did not know why we were there, or the whereabouts of her mother. The house was normal in appearance and was the largest house that I had been in during my time in San Diego. I was angered that criminals would be able to afford much nicer and more spacious living accommodations than the tiny apartment that my government salary as an FBI agent afforded us. This was certainly not the last time that this thought would cross my mind.

Agents with machine guns carefully cleared out the residence, and then the search portion of the operation began, as we had obtained both arrest and search warrants. The teenage girl was instructed to call her mother and tell her to come home, and her mother complied with her request. As soon as the mother showed up and pulled into the driveway, agents arrested her, placed her in handcuffs, and drove her back to the main FBI office so that she could be questioned along with the other subjects whom were being arrested that day.

For the search I played the role of photographer. This was

much more familiar and comfortable territory for me. With the extreme danger element over, I enjoyed being at a crime scene and having the opportunity to amass the photographic evidence as part of the operation. Experienced agents helped place number "tents" that marked the location of the pieces of evidence. I thoroughly documented the condition of the house before we entered. All hands searched the house for relevant evidence, and I continued to take photos in support of the operation. I took the photos in each room, and then as agents found evidence, I would take pictures of the evidence. In the meantime, I also had the opportunity to do some searching of my own in some areas of the house.

Searching through someone's personal property gave me an uncomfortable, prying feeling. I had always been taught to respect personal privacy and space, including possessions, and my built-in moral compass told me that it was wrong to dig through other people's things. Of course in this case the court had allowed us to perform the search, and we were looking for evidence that could help put a criminal behind bars. But I still had a wary feeling when opening drawers, looking under beds, and searching through the owner's possessions.

While searching in the garage, I came across a stash of "adult" related items, including leather outfits, whips, and other "adult" toys. This further compounded the feeling that I was invading someone's privacy. It helped me personally to realize the importance of limiting searches and to appreciate our basic rights afforded by the U.S. Constitution, which protect citizens from illegal searches and seizures. I could now easily visualize how a police state where law enforcement and the military can just walk into anyone's home would truly limit freedom. To me, the greatest core principles of the United States are our freedoms and privacy. In the searches I performed I respected privacy as much as possible, and I absolutely never did share comments or jokes about the possessions that we were searching through with other agents. I felt that all of the agents I worked with tried to follow the same overall search principles that I did. However, over time I would find that during some searches conducted with uniformed police officers, there were isolated incidences of crude remarks and jokes made during searches. To me this did not demonstrate the professionalism that most FBI agents and other federal law enforcement personnel showed. After a few hours, we completed our search and walked away with documents that established the relationship of the woman we arrested with the corrupt customs agent at the border.

We heard on the FBI radio that the primary arrest subject's location was still unknown, and that the other arrest team was not successful. This was considered to be a high risk arrest scenario, largely due to the fact that the subject was a trained federal agent with law enforcement tactics and firearms training. That is certainly not the type of person that I wanted to get into a gunfight with. The SWAT team had been deployed to perform the arrest of the main subject due to the high risk of violence. When they could not locate the subject, the FBI used surveillance including vehicles and air support. He had changed his work schedule, which led agents to fear that someone had tipped him off. However, later in the day the subject finally returned home and was arrested by the FBI without further incident. To me this arrest was particularly interesting because it was law enforcement arresting law enforcement. I wondered what the dynamics would be during the arrest. I wondered what the experience would be like talking to someone who was supposed to be on our side, but who had defected to the other side. Little did I know that I soon would have a major case involving a law enforcement officer who had gone bad.

On the surface, the arrest and search was fun and rewarding. I arrived at home exhausted; I had been up early, had adrenaline pumping, and had been in a stressful situation that I was not used to dealing with. I later realized how extremely relieved I was that it was over, but I was also proud to have participated on the arrest team and helped bring criminals to justice.

CHAPTER 27

Run for the Border

One of my first occasions to visit the San Ysidro international border crossing, which separates San Diego and Tijuana, was due to a fatal shooting involving ICE and a drug cartel. Late on a Wednesday afternoon I was notified about the incident. One of the violations that my squad was responsible for investigating was assaults on the federal officers, which were always referred to as "AFOs." We did not know any details except that there had been a shooting that had resulted in the death of a subject. Our supervisor directed three of us to head to the border, to report back on the situation, and then to receive further instructions. I ran out of the FBI office, hopped in my car, and sped towards the border (every time I made the drive to the border, I could not help but think of the popular Taco Bell slogan at the time, which was "Make a run for the border!").

The San Diego office is located about fifteen miles north of the border. The busiest border vehicle crossing in the world is the San Ysidro crossing where Interstate 5 runs into Mexico. As I sped down I-5, I could see that traffic was backed up worse than usual. Over the radio I learned that the entire border crossing point had been shut down. This meant that there would be tens of thousands of stranded motorists waiting for the border to reopen.

FBI cars typically have a siren and flashing lights, which FBI agents rarely have the opportunity to use. However, in this case, I was directed to use all means necessary to get to the border ASAP, including using my car's flashing lights and siren. I took great pleasure in flipping on the lights, turning on the siren, and driving on the shoulder and even the median at high speed. I was enjoying my drive like a kid enjoys speeding along on a shiny new bike down the street for the first time.

As I flew down the highway passing, thousands of stopped cars, I finally reached a point where traffic had been diverted off of the Interstate, leaving the final few miles to the border free of all vehicles. I took out my badge, slowed down, and without stopping I was motioned through by the California Highway Patrol to the eerily empty multi-lane Interstate highway to continue my journey to the crime scene. I had several miles of I-5 completely to myself, and I had a valid reason to speed. So I sped. For any driver to have miles of traffic-fee Interstate, especially for one of the busiest highways in the nation, is indeed a rare treat that I likely will never see again. I successfully tried to just enjoy the moment, and tried not to think about the stress and uncertainty of the situation that awaited me when I arrived at the border.

As I rolled up to the crime scene at the San Ysidro border, I showed my credentials to a group of officers who were engaged in what appeared to be an intense discussion. This border crossing is a gigantic complex that stretches across several acres, and features an extended pedestrian bridge for foot traffic, with dozens of lanes for traffic outbound from the United States and Mexico. Incoming traffic lanes are even more numerous, with seemingly countless booths that accompany each lane. The entry into the United States must be something akin to entering Disney World for those who legally pass through this particular crossing location. I found an empty parking space, located my senior training agent, and learned the details of the incident.

As we wandered into the vicinity of the crime scene, we walked past rows of cars that were stranded and unable to be moved because they were considered to be part of the crime scene. I also saw dozens of drivers who were being held as potential witnesses to the shooting. We continued to stroll along the line of cars until we entered an area commonly referred to as "no man's land," which is a small strip of land that is approximately fifty yards in width. This buffer zone sits directly between the United States and Mexico, and technically does not fall under the jurisdiction of either country. As we walked up to an area concentrated with law enforcement officials, I saw a sport utility vehicle that was bullet-ridden, with the driver's door ajar, and a body hanging out of the driver's seat with arms dangling into the roadway. Clearly the driver had been shot and killed in this fatal incident. I had previously never seen a real dead body "in the flesh" outside of a funeral home. Despite being exposed to numerous videos at the FBI Academy that depicted horrific fatal accidents, and even though I had watched several of the 80s Faces of Death (reality "gore") movies, this was a new, creepy, and sobering experience for me. I have the same or slightly greater morbid curiosity that most people have; I was tempted to gawk and stare as if I were a member of the general public driving by a tragic accident. But after a very brief view of the scene, out of respect for the dead, and to uphold the professionalism of being an FBI agent, I turned my attention away from the body and began to work with my fellow agents to scope out the aspects of what our role would be in this investigation.

The simple fact that the vehicle's position was in "no man's land" could have created significant legal and jurisdictional issues between the United States and Mexico. In this case, the vehicle was physically positioned closer to the United States border, and I surmised that the Mexican authorities, who were also observing the scene from their side of the fence, did not want to have anything to do with this mess. It was amazing to me that only a few feet separated the American agents from their Mexican counterparts, but working directly with each other would be very difficult because of the language barrier. This was the first of many occasions that I would see not only physical but language and cultural barriers that separate the two countries, and in light of the drug-related violence that has resulted in the death of tens of thousands of Mexican citizens, having barriers to isolate the United States from Mexico did not seem to be a bad thing under the circumstances.

As details emerged, we learned that there were several overlapping investigative jurisdictions, including the San Diego Police Department, San Diego Sheriff's Department, US Border Patrol, Immigration and Customs Enforcement (ICE), and the Federal Bureau of Investigation. The FBI typically is the lead agency for shared investigations, especially when crimes are border-related and involve federal agents. However, in this situation, no federal agents were injured, and due to the nature of the shooting and the responding organizations, the case quickly developed into an effort lead by the San Diego Police Department, with the primary federal assistance coming from ICE.

While the FBI tends to dominate the imagination of the media and the press, the reality is that more specialized law enforcement agencies are often much better equipped to handle some investigations, such as this shooting,. The FBI is efficient at coordinating massive large-scale disaster response across multiple agencies, but for specific criminal cases the FBI frequently offers a supportive role rather than directly performing investigative steps. Police deal with shootings on a daily basis, and while this particular instance involved federal agents, the circumstances were not unusual and logically fell within the investigative territory of the San Diego Police Department. As representatives of the FBI, we were happy to stand aside and let the cops do their work, which would not only yield a high quality investigative process, but would expedite opening this critical border crossing up. In chatting with some of the Border Patrol agents, we found that they were amazed to see the border crossing closed; none of them had ever seen this happen during their entire careers. They reported that the only other time the crossing had closed was the day John F. Kennedy had been assassinated in 1963.

We also began to learn more details of the shooting from the Border Patrol agent witnesses. Apparently a drug runner had driven across the border coming from Mexico into the United States. An undercover narcotics unit had gained intelligence on this vehicle, and our agents had slipped in behind the vehicle and followed it as it drove into United States. The driver of the suspect's vehicle apparently "made" (spotted) the undercover car, and elected to turn around and try to head back to the safety of Mexico. He exited the highway, crossed an overpass, and began to head back southbound on Interstate 5. At this point the agents in the undercover unit realized that the offender was trying to get back into Mexico, so they radioed ahead to agents at the border and alerted them to try to stop the vehicle before it could re-enter Mexico. When leaving the United States at the San Ysidro crossing, the lanes from Interstate 5 feed directly into Mexico without having any physical barriers or checkpoints. The United States does not limit who is leaving the country; traffic is only slowed by scattered concrete barricades that physically separate the lanes right before they enter Mexico. In this instance, the agents quickly fanned out between the lanes of traffic and began to look for the vehicle that was approaching. The agents spotted the vehicle, waived their arms, drew their weapons, and shouted for the driver of the vehicle to come to a stop. The driver knew that he would be home free if he could just make it across the border, so he made the fateful decision not to stop. The agents who were on foot did not benefit from the usual protection of guard stations. They were confronted with the life-threatening situation of having an approaching vehicle that was being used as a deadly weapon against them.

It is impossible to know with complete certainty if the driver of this vehicle intended to try to kill agents, or if he merely thought that the agents would jump out of the way and allow him to enter Mexico. Regardless of the driver's intent, the agents opened fire on the driver when it appeared that there was an eminent threat of death or serious bodily injury to themselves or others in the vicinity. The driver's door was pummeled with gunfire from agents, the vehicle coasted to a stop in the no man's land area between the two countries, the driver managed to open his door, and he slumped to the ground as he drew his final breath. The extreme violence of the shooting made a huge impression on me, and probably contributed to my recurring nightmares involving shootings and death.

This shooting was my introduction to the violent Mexican criminal element that is associated with drug smuggling. It is an ugly business, and numerous people get killed, ranging from innocent citizens to drug cartel members. Big money is at stake (in the tens or even hundreds of billions of US dollars), and the cartels do not hesitate to take action to cash in on the multitude of high risk but high reward illegal opportunities that are available. This incident was also my first exposure to how criminals use the Mexican border to their advantage as a shield or safety net; they can commit a crime in the United States and then easily escape by simply getting back into Mexico. I would see this pattern repeated numerous times during my term in San Diego.

After spending several hours standing around and relaying messages back to our supervisor and management at the FBI field office we wrapped up the evening. The news media was present, complete with reporters and helicopters, and it was interesting to be part of the scene and gain an insider's perspective. I always thought that an event such as this one would be an enjoyable part of being an FBI agent. It definitely separated the job of being an agent from the average day job spent in a cubicle. But as the hours slowly piled on, one after another, my excitement at the crime scene diminished and I longed for my wife, pets, and comfortable bed. I finally trudged through my apartment door well after midnight, scarfed down some food, and went to bed to sleep a few hours before the challenges of the next day began.

CHAPTER 28

Big Bear Prison Transport

FBI agents do not have nine-to-five jobs. Criminals do not work "business hours." That is a given that is understood by everyone who enters the profession. But what I did not realize was that there would be days that would begin as early as 2:00 a.m. and end long after the sun went down. And some days would last for two sunrises, without a wink of sleep in between. Just a couple of months after arriving in San Diego, I had the opportunity to experience one of these extended long days.

The FBI has investigative authority over many different violations, ranging from bank robberies, to kidnapping, to terrorism. Compared to violations that other agencies work, the FBI is incredibly broad in scope. Often, jurisdiction of criminal matters between the FBI and other entities overlaps. If the investigation is purely related to drugs, then it is typically headed by DEA. However, there are often cases that involve a number of different criminal charges, and usually these more complex and varied investigations are performed by the FBI. Depending on the evidence that is available, the FBI often works with the US Attorney to aggressively pursue charges that are not immediately related to the primary offense. For example, for organized crime cases, there may be drug charges and related charges that can be applied. However, frequently the FBI relies on wire fraud and mail fraud charges to put criminals behind bars. The FBI takes the common sense viewpoint that it does not matter technically what the offense is; as long as bad guys are off the streets; that is what is important.

The FBI in San Diego had a long-term investigation of gang activity. One gang in particular was known to be funding their operations through transport and sale of methamphetamines, simply referred to as meth. Meth has moved to dominating the illegal drug trade, much like crack cocaine ruled the drugs of the 80s and 90s. Meth has already destroyed an untold numbers of lives, probably numbering in the millions, either through addiction, serious injury, or death. One of the biggest impacts of meth is that many people across the United States have elected to create their own meth labs, resulting in horrific chemical burns and sometimes death, not only for themselves, but family members, innocent bystanders, and law-enforcement officials. TV shows popularize the notion of "average Americans" getting their cut of the drug trade; *Weeds* and *Breaking Bad* were two of my favorite shows that dealt with the topic. But fiction is one thing; the reality and raw harshness that surrounds the illegal drug trade is not something any "average American" would want any part of if he or she were adequately informed of the inherent dangers of this lifestyle.

For this particular case, the FBI had identified approximately thirty subjects who were known to deal meth. Arrest warrants were obtained and a date was set to round up the criminals. One of the arrest warrants issued was for a female in her late 20s who was living in the Big Bear Lake vicinity in California. Big Bear is located approximately two hours northeast of Los Angeles in the San Bernardino Mountains. It is a common vacation destination for many Southern Californians, known for having a beautiful lake set amidst the gorgeous Sierra Nevada Mountains. The area has a reputation for having an outdoorsy "vacation getaway" feel, which is quite the opposite of the usual criminal setting of poverty-stricken inner-city neighborhoods. While other agents were tasked with searches and arrests in the San Diego area, I was selected by my superiors to participate on the Big Bear arrest team.

The arrest plan called for the arrest team to convene in Big Bear at 4:30 in the morning. Multiple people from multiple agencies, including the San Bernardino County Sheriff's Department and the Los Angeles Division of the FBI, would participate in the arrest. The San Diego FBI would ultimately be in charge of the arrests and related searches. My part of the plan involved arresting one of the female subjects, and then providing the in-custody escort and transportation for her back to San Diego, where she would face charges. I was assigned to work with a fellow female agent working at the North San Diego County satellite office. We agreed to meet at 2:00 a.m. so we would have ample time to make the lengthy drive to arrive in Big Bear on time. Although I lived close to the office, I had to wake up by 1:30 a.m. to get geared up and be on time. I knew I was in for a full day, entailing hours of driving, a high-pressure arrest scenario, an intense and important search of the property, and finally a lengthy prisoner transport.

At 2:00 a.m. we departed for Big Bear from San Diego. We drove for a couple of hours on I-15 and then exited and took smaller mountain roads to the higher altitude of Big Bear. After locating our rendezvous point at the local sheriff's station, we convened with other law enforcement officials and determined our final arrest plan. For this arrest I borrowed another agent's shotgun, and was assigned to a position at the back of the subject's property in case anyone tried to flee. Arrests like this are intimidating because an agent simply does not know what unexpected scenario could play out. The FBI tries to plan ahead by researching all of the residents of a property where a search or arrest will occur to make sure that there are no outstanding warrants; however, criminals are often transient and hang out at other criminals' houses. Although most arrests occur smoothly and without incident, agents never know when they are going to come across a wanted violent criminal that they had not planned on encountering.

When the clock struck six a.m., we drove up rapidly but quietly to the arrest site, and agents silently exited the vehicles and prepared to enter the property. This particular arrest scenario was unusual in that there were two houses on one lot, one large and one small, which formed a small compound. Surrounded by trees, it evoked images of similar locations I had seen where outcomes had been fatal for law enforcement and the criminals whom they were attempting to arrest. Wearing my bulletproof vest, with a shotgun in hand, I felt prepared and incredibly alert. I ensured that I had a round in the chamber of the shotgun, and placed my finger lightly on the safety. In an effort to make the least amount of noise possible, I stepped lightly and took up a position behind the primary residence on the property with my shotgun barrel pointing to a double glass door.

Shortly after taking my position, I heard shouting and demands of the FBI being issued to the residents to open the door and come out with their hands up. I waited anxiously, envisioning a crazy drugged-out person who could come crashing through the glass window at any time with a machine gun ready to open fire. But nothing of any particular danger or excitement happened in this arrest, which is the normal occurrence for FBI arrests. The residents included an older couple, along with the subject whom we were arresting. In addition, there was a young girl who appeared to be the subject's daughter. All parties seemed perplexed that the FBI was there, and at a glance, nobody in this family seemed to be a hardened criminal type.

We arrested and secured the subject, and then began a methodical search of the property. I volunteered to perform the role of taking crime scene photos, and I helped to organize the search, room by room. The search was for evidence of drugs; however, after several hours we found very little evidence that would be useful in court. The subject was arrested for transporting one pound of meth to drug dealers in San Diego. That had been several months ago, and the subject claimed not to have returned to the San Diego vicinity since then. Based on the lack of evidence at her property, it seemed to me that the subject had probably steered clear of criminal activity recently. But unfortunately for her, a past lapse in judgment had caught up with her.

We wrapped up the search, and it was time to head back to San Diego with our prisoner. FBI standard operating procedure for transporting criminals includes cuffing the prisoners' hands behind their backs. This can be quite uncomfortable, even for a short period of time. In this case, we tried to allow as much comfort as possible while fulfilling the FBI's requirements. The plan was for me to drive while my partner rode in the back seat with the prisoner. If the prisoner attempted to cause trouble or escape, this activity would be immediately noticed and corrected by the agent in the back seat. The FBI has the policy of having an agent sit in the back seat with prisoners during transport because there have been multiple cases of prisoners who free themselves in the back seat of a police car, and then injure or kill the officers who are transporting them. I was not overly concerned about our prisoner, who seemed more tired and confused than threatening. I will never forget the sheer devastation on her face as we took her away in handcuffs in front of her family, including her daughter. If this scene and raw emotions could be conveyed to potential future criminals, that would probably set them straight where all other methods fail.

We began to drive back down the twisty mountain roads, heading from Big Bear to San Diego. Following FBI procedure, we radioed to the San Diego office and informed agents of our time and mileage. After driving about ten miles, I noticed the heat indicator on the dashboard was showing that the engine was extremely overheated. I could not believe how unfortunate and unlucky this was; I had followed all instructions and training to the letter, but was confronted with a situation that I did not know how to handle. But part of the training we received was focused on how to handle any surprise that arises; namely, "do the right thing" and use common sense. So I informed my partner that the car was overheating, and if we continued, permanent engine damage would occur. I then found a side road with an open gravel area next to the road, and pulled into that location. A massive amount of steam erupted from the car; clearly there was a serious problem that was beyond my ability to fix on the spot. I pressed the button on my microphone and tried to radio for help, but there was no response; we were out of range due to the hills and valleys of the surrounding terrain. As a last resort, my partner and I each attempted to use our cell phones to call for help, and again we were met with failure; all communications were in a "dead zone."

There was nothing else to do but wait for the other agents to drive by as they were returning to San Diego. So she could be comfortable, we pulled the prisoner out of the back seat and let her stretch her legs. Now that we were out of the car, I walked a few yards to the highest spot I could find, and while literally standing on my toes I managed to get a cell signal. I conducted a quick and garbled call to the San Diego FBI office and informed them of the situation. They said to hang tight and promised to radio for help from other agents immediately.

We had time to kill before help arrived. The scene was no doubt memorable to anyone who happened to drive by; there was a woman in handcuffs, with two FBI agents standing guard, complete with a car with the hood popped open and steam slowly rising. Several cars slowed, and one person offered to assist. We motioned people forward with a smile, and thought to myself that this was certainly not something that would have happened with my old corporate job. While I figured that someday I would look back and laugh, I still was still nervous and concerned that something else would go wrong. I certainly had not anticipated having this much excitement as part of my first prisoner transport in which I was the driver.

Other agents finally arrived, much to our relief. We swapped out vehicles with the other agents and continued our journey. As soon as we got into radio range, I was able to talk with the personnel at San Diego. I told them the whole story of my vehicle breaking down, causing the delay. I could hear laughter and excitement in the background back at the office, because they knew I was a new agent and had really been challenged with an unusual scenario. Even for seasoned FBI agents, transporting prisoners is not a frequent occurrence. To be a new agent and to experience a vehicle breakdown while transporting a prisoner through the mountains and to have been out of communication during the ordeal was an experience that few agents share.

My partner and I talked with the prisoner on the several hour drive back to San Diego. We were not probing for information or a confession; we just wanted to ease some of the pain and anguish that she was going through. I told her that I liked the Big Bear area and that I planned to show the area to my wife, and asked her about what types of recreational activities were available and if she had any lodging recommendations. While our prisoner was not extremely talkative, I do think she enjoyed a little bit of light conversation to help ease her mind and let her know that even though the FBI had arrested her, we would treat her with the fairness and respect that she or any other citizen deserves. As with most prisoners, she wanted to know the specific charges she was facing, and what the maximum sentence was for those charges. I shared with her as much information as I knew and treated her exactly like I would want to be treated if our roles were reversed. I explained to her that she had been arrested for transporting of drugs, and I explained that I did not know for sure what type of prison sentence she could be facing. But I did share that I had heard word-of-mouth that for her offense that she could get up to ten years, although there tends to be a great degree of variability with sentencing, assuming that the case makes it to that point.

To some degree, as I would on other occasions for other subjects who I helped to arrest, I felt sorry for her and hoped that she could get a reduced sentence. She had a family, had been staying in Big Bear without any trouble, was holding a legitimate job, and seemed to have her life on track. However, she was about to be pulled back into the justice system; prisons have a way of keeping people in trouble permanently, even after they have served their time. Facing felony charges, her future did not look bright; depending on the sentence, her daughter would almost be an adult by the time she would be released. The reality was that the subject had tried to make some quick, easy money, and was going to pay the price for her bad judgment.

We finally made it to San Diego, were greeted with smiles from an array of FBI employees who had heard about our ordeal of breaking down, and dropped off our prisoner for further processing. My parting words to our prisoner were simply "good luck." I truly meant it. As with many cases and criminals that I encountered, I never learned the final outcome of her case, but I wished her the best.

CHAPTER 29

FBI SWAT

The FBI San Diego Division has a SWAT (Special Weapons and Tactics) team, used for arrests with a high degree of danger and violence. An FBI SWAT team consists of about twenty agents from various squads with a wide range of experience levels. These agents, all of whom are in excellent physical and mental condition, are required to undergo special physical and firearms handling requirements that are above and beyond the already high levels established for regular FBI agents. The SWAT team members have an incredible level of dedication. They go through a rigorous training regimen and are almost always on-call for a variety of potential situations that can develop, including arrests, barricaded subjects, and other hazardous situations. During my time in San Diego, the team, which had previously been headed up by my squad supervisor, had several team members from my squad.

After chatting with SWAT team members, I had an urge to see the team in action, so I voluntarily elected to assist the SWAT team with an arrest. The subject of the arrest, who was considered to be armed and dangerous, was a gang member, and merited an arrest approach using the careful planning and execution that the SWAT team offered. My assignment was to arrive in visual range of the house of the gang member in a location that would not be conspicuous, yet would allow me to keep watch on the house continuously. I was to look for signs of activity, such as a moving curtain, lights being turned on or off, or anyone entering or leaving the premises through doors or windows. The arrest was to occur at 6:00 a.m., so I arrived with a fellow agent who was a SWAT team member over an hour in advance to keep watch on the arrest location. While most agents do not get the opportunity to watch a SWAT team operate, I was fortunate to participate and to listen in on the SWAT radio frequency as the arrest was executed.

We carefully observed the house, an activity which is literally called "having the eye." We saw no movement inside, so as the arrest time approached, my partner radioed back to the staging area for the SWAT team that there was no activity in the house and that the operation was a "go." Over the radio we heard SWAT team commands instructing agents to load up in their vehicles and drive to the scene. We continued to keenly view the house; we knew that if we failed to spot a prepared and armed criminal, that could result in a fatal day for the SWAT team members. But the morning was quiet and we saw no activity; there was nothing else for us to do except enjoy being in a fantastic position to sit back and watch the show. Within a few minutes we witnessed multiple large SUVs loom out of the darkness. We caught a glimpse of more SUVs quickly rolling through the alley behind the house, images which were exactly what most people envision as the typical FBI arrest. For me it was an absolute thrill, and seeing the action unfold was better than having a front row seat in a theater with 3-D.

Agents, fully geared with matching outfits, goggles, helmets, and assault weapons, flew from their vehicles in orchestrated fashion. I was giddy with anticipation, knowing a criminal was about to have the rudest wake-up in his life. The agents quietly and quickly moved in lines next to the doors and windows and prepared for the arrest.

Following FBI protocol, an agent rapped on the front door and yelled out a command for the occupants of the house to immediately open the door and come out with their hands up. I could clearly hear the commands from a hundred yards away with my vehicle's windows rolled up. There was still no activity from the house, which meant the next steps in the arrest process were about to get much more interesting.

SWAT teams often make "dynamic entries," which means team members go into the criminal's turf to make an arrest. Dynamic entries are extremely dangerous compared to other arrest scenarios. Potentially subjects can be awake and merely waiting for law enforcement to enter their premises, a situation which can easily be deadly for the arresting officers or agents. The advantage with a non-dynamic arrest is that law enforcement is safely positioned and simply has to wait for the person to come out with his or her hands up. But the disadvantage of a lengthy non-dynamic arrest is that the subjects have plenty of time to think about their predicament, which increases the odds that they will grab weapons and respond violently to the threat, law enforcement, who wants to take away their personal freedom, in the form of an arrest. Innocent bystanders or occupants can be injured or killed in this scenario. Therefore, depending on the background and mindset of a subject, a dynamic arrest can potentially offer a safer alternative than "waiting out" a subject. Another advantage of a dynamic arrest is that subjects are not given time to conceal a crime by destroying evidence. That is incredibly important, because without evidence, a criminal who cannot be prosecuted due to lack of evidence will be back on the streets, and will almost always continue to be involved in criminal activities. The decision on how to conduct an arrest is one of the numerous difficult judgment calls that are frequently made by FBI agents. In hindsight, the right decision always seems clear, but prior to an arrest, the best and safest route is only an educated guess.

We continued to watch the SWAT team members and saw the agents unloading a battering ram that would be used to force entry into the property. Next, the agent with the ram took a huge swing at the front door and cracked it open on the first attempt. The other SWAT team members swarmed into the house, and almost without breathing, we listened to the radio traffic crackle with activity. Watching the SWAT team members in action was exhilarating, and I could feel a slight wave of adrenaline as they performed their dangerous work. And I was sitting safely behind the wheel of my car, without exposure to any danger. I could only imagine what those guys were feeling; I assumed it was an addictive and powerful mixture of fear and aggression. While my violent crime squad performed dangerous activities, it was nothing compared to the extreme hazards that SWAT teams are frequently subjected to. I loved watching the SWAT team in action but was glad to be in the crowd and not onstage.

Over the radio we could hear some confusion developing; it sounded as if the subject had not been arrested, and the house still had locked doors. Only a matter of seconds after digesting this news, we heard and felt a massive boom that originated from the arrest property. The sound was so loud that the floorboard of our vehicle vibrated and the images in the mirrors briefly blurred. The FBI SWAT team had just used a flash grenade, which is a device intended to stun subjects and put them at a disadvantage in an arrest situation. The grenade successfully stunned the subject and helped the SWAT team members finish their jobs; a short time later we saw the subject being led out of the house in handcuffs.

The arrest was a great success; no criminals, FBI agents, or innocent bystanders had been hurt. I was impressed with the efficiency, precision, and judgment that the SWAT team had displayed, and I could see that almost any person who decided to go up against the SWAT team was going to come out on the losing end.

CHAPTER 30

German Rapper

In the course of my work as an FBI agent, I encountered an unusual bank robber. The FBI learned through an informant the possible identity of the subject, who had robbed several banks using takeover-style tactics. A combination of video evidence and the informant's information pointed us to the robber's identity, although we did not have sufficient evidence to arrest him and be absolutely confident that he would be convicted. The FBI began surveillance so we could learn more about the patterns the robber followed, such as where he went during the day and during the evening, and whom he associated with regularly. We would be ready if he tried to strike again before we had time to build a rock-solid case for his arrest. My squad, which was responsible for bank robbery investigations, was also responsible for the surveillance. We began our operations and watched him for a period of several days. Some of our technical experts placed a tracking device on his vehicle, which was a "tricked out" (or "pimped out," as many would say) Mercedes sedan. This was an appropriate vehicle for our subject to drive; he turned out to be a German-born rapper.

As we surveiled the subject and watched his erratic patterns, we became increasingly concerned that he would attempt to rob another bank. We reached a decision that the FBI SWAT team would be placed on continuous alert, and if the subject came within the vicinity of a bank, the SWAT team would be called to action. Bank robberies are notoriously dangerous, especially when involving subjects who are armed and rob the bank "takeover style." In 1986, in Miami, Florida, one of the worst tragedies in FBI history occurred when agents attempted to apprehend bank robbers immediately after a robbery, and several agents wound up losing their lives. A surviving agent from the gun battle that had erupted in Miami spoke to my class at Quantico and painted a sobering picture of the reality and dangers of arrest scenarios involving armed robbers.

We conducted surveillance for several days. Late one morning, we observed the subject heading to the Point Loma area of San Diego. This area has several bank branches, all of which seemed to be likely targets. My partner and I positioned ourselves outside of a bank, with fellow agents from my squad taking up positions in the vicinity. The SWAT team arrived and staged several blocks away. We were ready for a robbery if the subject decided to take action.

The main subject and his accomplice were spotted parking a few blocks away. They walked to a position across the street from the bank and appeared to be studying the entrance. I could see them and announced this activity over the radio; everyone was on high alert. The subjects positioned themselves directly behind my squad mate's vehicle, which happened to be occupied by my squad mate as part of the surveillance operation. We breathlessly monitored the suspects, hoping that they would not realize that they were being watched. Since we presumed they were armed, this situation was becoming extremely hazardous. While watching, I elected temporarily to not call out what I was seeing, since I did not want the subjects to hear radio traffic from my squad mate's car. After a long couple of minutes, they meandered down the street, and everyone breathed a short sigh of relief.

A few minutes passed. We witnessed the subjects walking back towards the entrance of the bank, except this time they were wearing hats and sunglasses. We knew what was about to go down. Radio calls were made and the FBI SWAT team was alerted. We were then faced with another dilemma; we could arrest the subjects in the bank, or we could allow the robbery to occur and let the subjects head back to their car, where they could be arrested. We knew that the robbers had been armed in previous robberies, yet they had not ever fired any shots or injured anybody. If we tried to arrest them in the bank, we could find ourselves in the middle of a hostage situation or worse; there could be a fatal shooting involving innocent bystanders. The difficult decision was made by the FBI leadership to allow the bank robbery to happen and then arrest the subjects afterwards.

About twenty to thirty seconds after walking into the building, the subjects came sprinting out. They had concealed their weapons, and were heading back to their Mercedes getaway car on foot. I could hardly believe that we had just witnessed a bank robbery, which fortunately had not resulted in any injuries or harm to the victims in the bank. Having previously seen the FBI SWAT SUVs driving on nearby streets, I knew that the subjects were about to have a little "reality check" with the SWAT guys.

The SWAT team was fully prepared to arrest the robbers in their vehicle. They allowed both thieves to get into the car, and then they team detonated a flash grenade on the roof of the car, which stunned both occupants. Both robbers were safely arrested; no one was hurt and once again the FBI SWAT team, in conjunction with my squad, had successfully handled a potentially violent situation. I would see the FBI handle numerous situations like this with an incredibly high success rate; most people only hear about the rare occurrences where things go awry, which is statistically certain to happen eventually, due to the high variability and dynamic nature of these types of arrests.

Later that day I was involved in some follow-up aspects of this investigation. I was picked to talk to the robber's mother to see if we could learn any more information about her son. Telling a mother that her son had been arrested for bank robbery was painful. She sobbed and I could see the absolute despair and failure written on her face. I tried to be as understanding and compassionate as possible, which I knew she appreciated. That evening I transported the prisoner to the federal prison in downtown San Diego. I talked to him and he tried to talk his way out of going to prison; I had to give him an "A" for effort. He said that the FBI did not understand the whole picture, and that he was just trying to protect his girlfriend who had supposedly gone missing. He claimed that he robbed the bank so that he could get ransom money to free his kidnapped girlfriend. We knew that this was a lie, and he provided no details about her name, where she lived, or what her telephone number was. After reminding him that it is illegal and punishable by five years in prison to lie to an FBI agent, he stopped providing bogus information. The reality that he had reached the end of his glamorous "gangster rap" lifestyle was apparent as we waited outside of the prison for the gate to open. I told him to hang tough and wished him luck when we handed him over to the federal prison authorities.

CHAPTER 31

Arrest at the Car Dealership

Another case that I worked was aimed at arresting a serial criminal who was wanted for a lengthy string of bank robberies in the San Diego area. The FBI's standard practice when investigating bank robberies was to obtain security camera photos from banks that were robbed, which we aired on the local television stations. On one gorgeous San Diego Friday afternoon, we got lucky and received a call from a salesman at a car dealership who had just provided a test drive to a man who looked like the robber and who had inquired about paying cash for a car. This suspect was planning on returning to the car dealer the following day to complete a purchase of a vehicle.

That night I worked with the San Diego PD and my squad to formulate a plan on how to arrest the subject. We knew an approximate time that the subject would return to the dealer on Saturday, so we decided to perform a joint arrest operation at the dealership. While this would pose some potential risk to bystanders, it allowed us to carefully plan and prepare for the arrest, which was the most desirable and predictable scenario for us.

The FBI team reconvened late Saturday morning, and then received notification from the car dealer saying that the subject had called to say he was going to be at the dealership around noon, which was two hours earlier than we were expecting. A glance at our watches showed that the time was already 11:00 a.m.; we still had work to do to get prepared and in place, so we all ran to our cars, flipped on our police radios, rushed to the vicinity of the car dealership, and began our final coordination for planning the arrest. The plan was for the salesman to be on the lookout for the subject, and once he saw the subject arrive to get out of the way and allow the San Diego PD and FBI to perform the arrest. My role was to sit inside the car dealership, along with my partner, and ensure that the customers would be safe. We would be ready to lock doors, push customers under desks, and worst-case, we would be armed and ready for a shootout if things went awry. The subject had displayed firearms during the commission of his robberies, so there was a risk of a violent outcome.

My partner that day was Special Agent Janet Pardee, a small woman in stature but one of the most confident, knowledgeable, and capable agents I ever met; she was only a class behind me at the FBI Academy but quickly gained experience, making her an invaluable asset for the Bureau. Janet and I went inside the dealership and quickly took inventory of the surroundings.

As we waited inside the dealership, a member of the FBI surveillance team spotted the subject driving up. I moved quickly to lock the doors of the dealership, and told customers and staff to head to the back of the building. Janet had a vantage point that allowed her to view the subject and the arrest, and she told me to get down. I crouched behind a thin wall with my hand on my weapon; I was ready to act if needed. The arrest was made safely and without incident.

I later learned from one of the San Diego PD detectives that the robber had put his finger on the trigger of his gun. This meant that the detective had reached a point during the arrest at which the subject was not cooperating, and the detective had almost reached the difficult but split-second decision to use lethal force. The subject initially refused to put his hands up, and for a moment appeared to be reaching into his waistband for a weapon. Based on my positioning behind the subject, if the detective had pulled the trigger, I would have been in his line of fire, and potentially the line of fire from other agents, if a gunfight had erupted.

A news station had intercepted the police radio transmission and was aware that we were about to arrest a bank robber. There were news cameras that rolled up to the scene as the arrest was taking place; I would later see myself on the news, at least for a brief moment. I was proud, knowing that I had taken part in an operation that successfully removed an armed and dangerous man from the streets.

CHAPTER 32

Sources

FBI agents are in the information business. Information is what leads to new cases, which leads to arrests, which leads to trials, which leads to prison sentences, which ultimately results in a safer society. Clearly with 9/11 permanently seared in the collective minds of the citizens of the United States, the result of what happens when information is not gathered or effectively shared is painfully evident. In recognition of the importance of information and intelligence gathering, the FBI requires all agents to operate at least one active source of information, who is called an informant.

The FBI Academy curriculum spends a deservedly significant amount of time instructing new agents on the vast number of rules and policies governing how sources are handled within the FBI. I relished the afternoon training classes in which we learned about informants, including the huge intelligence victories the FBI has benefitted from, and dramatic intelligence failures that resulted in secrets lost to cold war enemies. We were taught examples of embarrassing situations involving romantic links of FBI agents with their sources, which is strictly forbidden. In one extreme example, we learned about an agent who murdered his informant, whom he happened to be sleeping with, because he did not want his family to discover his secret. Another story involved an agent who was romantically linked to a source from China, who turned out to be a spy for the Chinese government. FBI agents generally are the brightest and most honest group of people in the world, but there have been several outrageously rotten apples that have been detrimental to the FBI's reputation and the nation's security.

Due to a plethora of rules and accompanying administrative steps that are required when running a source, stacks of paperwork were generated, even for a brief meeting with a source. The administrative overhead was a deterrent to agents for operating sources who were not beneficial to the FBI, and in some cases were a deterrent to operating sources, period, regardless of their potential benefit to the agency. Some agents on my squad absolutely despised the idea of having to operate a source. They reasoned that since we were on a reactive violent crime squad, we had no business trying to operate sources. While I understood that argument, I felt that we were frequently in a position to deal with lower-level criminals, and that compared to other FBI agents, we were in a unique and advantageous position to get fruitful intelligence from a wide cast of characters. While many of the sources were not exactly model citizens, I realized that they could help us capture other criminals, and that we might even find inroads to get inside information on organized crime, drug cartels, and other areas that provide the greatest threats to our country.

I looked forward to finding sources; I was proud to represent the FBI and give citizens the opportunity to help us help make the country a better place. My first opportunity to work a source arose one afternoon when I was answering telephones as the FBI agent on duty. A call came in regarding a tip about a wanted criminal who fled the United States and was residing in South America. The information was provided by a man who seemed to have a great deal of knowledge about drug related production and kidnappings. I decided to ask him if he was willing to participate as an information source for the FBI, and he readily agreed. I was thrilled to have my first source.

When meeting with sources, the FBI has a policy that an agent must always have an additional agent with him or her. This is necessary for several reasons. First, it provides additional safety in the event that a source turns violent. Second, it ensures that the information shared is heard by two agents; when reports are written out about the information that was shared, documentation of the meeting is more accurate and has a stronger legal basis since it was heard by two witnesses. Finally, it prevents agents from engaging in improper conduct with their sources.

My new source claimed to have family members who were directly tied to Colombian drug production organizations, and was in a position to potentially gain excellent intelligence on the source of much of the drug trafficking that impacts our nation. He also claimed to have knowledge about kidnappings in Colombia and other South American locations. Unfortunately, neither international drug production crimes nor international kidnapping cases (without US citizen involvement) were matters that my squad could address. At the initial sessions with the informant, he shared a significant amount of information, which I studiously documented in report form. I hoped that my work would eventually help take down criminals, or possibly help rescue a kidnapping victim.

However, I began to see over time that even with specific information, it was difficult to find agents who were willing to take on more work and pursue leads that my source generated, especially since most of the reported criminal activity was occurring outside of the United States. This was especially difficult to explain to my source, who was surprised at the lack of action that the FBI took based on the information he provided. My source was also hoping to be paid for his information, but since it did not result in any arrests, I was not able to justify any payments to him from the FBI.

I also served as a partner for other FBI agents when meeting with their sources. I always enjoyed these occasions; I enjoyed meeting people, especially ones who were trying to help the FBI. Some of the sources played significant roles in cases ranging from bank robberies to kidnappings.

Occasionally I had to work with sources that were usually

handled by other field offices, or other law enforcement entities. In one case, due to the high security necessary around to protect the identity of sources, I received a plain brown envelope from a special security courier that was stamped "For Your Eyes Only." I could not help but smile at the phrase, which happened to be the title of one of my favorite James Bond films. The days of working with sources, while not always productive, were at least enjoyable and exciting, and will always be a part of the FBI experience that I look back on fondly.

CHAPTER 33

Protection Detail

One of the most interesting assignments that I had was working protection detail for foreign visiting dignitaries and political party members. Based on the significant body of work of fiction related to this topic, I had preconceived notions on how protection details worked. Surely there would be motorcades of agents with machine guns, earpiece radios, helicopters, and snipers on top of buildings. However, I quickly learned that this was not quite the norm.

The Secret Service is responsible for the protection of certain people: the President of the United States, the Vice President, the families of the President and Vice President, and candidates for these offices. The Secret Service partners with multiple law enforcement agencies, including the FBI, to fulfill this mission. On several occasions, the San Diego office assigned me to be the lead agent to liaison with the Secret Service for these visits. I was responsible for coordinating intelligence gathered by the FBI that would raise awareness of potential threats to those protected by the Secret Service. Also, in the event of incidents such as a shooting or a bomb being detonated, I would be the lead agent in the FBI responsible for coordinating investigations and responses. I worked directly with Secret Service agents on these assignments.

While I never came across any legitimate threats during any of these visits, I thoroughly enjoyed learning about how things work behind the scenes. I was proud to see the memos that were sent out to all FBI agents in San Diego that would announce an upcoming visit from one of the leaders of the nation, and in the same message my name would be referenced as the agent to work with on any intelligence concerning credible threats.

During the summer of 2006, I was assigned as the lead agent responsible for the safety of the visiting Attorney General of Mexico, Daniel Cabeza de Vaca. At the height of Mexico's war on drugs, their Attorney General planned to come to San Diego and was scheduled to make a speech putting the drug cartels on notice that they would be aggressively pursued, and announcing the deployment of Mexican Army troops to help quell the violence. He was a high value and high risk target who would be tempting to the powerful drug cartels. He spent several days in San Diego, and the FBI was the sole law enforcement agency responsible for his protection. I coordinated getting an armored vehicle; having briefings with his personal staff and protection detail from Mexico; making hotel arrangements including adjoining rooms staffed by agents; and supervising advance preparations for each of his locations during the visit.

My supervisor had pulled me aside and told me, "While the Attorney General's safety is important, your safety is more important, and if bullets start flying, just protect yourself, even if that means jumping in the nearest ditch." Throughout the visit, I was armed and constantly wearing my vest, and I thought that if violence erupted, I would fall back on my training, which would be first to take cover, and then fight back. Fortunately, there were no threats during his visit. Regardless of expectations from my management, I felt an incredible sense of responsibility for the Attorney General's safety, and I was relieved to see him board his plane alive and with no bullet holes at the end of his journey.

During the several day visit, I had to devote all of my time, twenty-four hours per day, to the protection detail. Prior to being assigned to the protection detail, I had purchased tickets to see one of my most admired movie icons: Ray Harryhausen. He was speaking in San Diego about his stop-motion movie techniques and would be signing books and showing off some of his famous movie props. Since I had to miss the event, Jennifer went in my place and even managed to get a book signed for me. His death in 2013 saddened me; I will never get to meet the man responsible for creating films that fueled my childhood imagination. I saw how the FBI could be all-consuming, and felt bad for those who have to skip family events due to the demands of a career in the FBI: children's plays, graduations, and weddings are all at risk to be missed by FBI agents.

CHAPTER 34

Assaults on Federal Officers

The FBI famously was depicted in the *X Files* TV show as investigating UFOs and other strange phenomenon. While I would have been thrilled to be chasing UFOs, I unfortunately spent much of my time investigating what are called "AFOs", which stands for an Assault on a Federal Officer. While AFOs could involve any threat or harm to a federal official (including judges or employees of any federal agency), these investigations typically were related to Border Patrol or Immigration and Customs Enforcement agents who were attacked or assaulted when attempting to arrest illegal aliens.

Since my squad was located in San Diego right next to the border, we had a large number of AFOs to investigate. Most of my squad mates absolutely despised getting a call related to AFOs; it did not take long for me to experience first-hand the long hours and remote locations involved with these investigations.

AFO investigations are typically conducted first at the scene of the assault, and then at the nearest border patrol checkpoint, which usually has offices and holding stations where victims and suspects can both be interviewed. The incidents usually occur in areas where there is no border fence between Mexico and the United States. The fenced portion of the Mexican border with California stretches from the Pacific Ocean for a number of miles eastward through the populated border areas around San Ysidro and Chula Vista, and is an effective deterrent to illegal crossings and activity. It is heavily patrolled and monitored, making illegal entry difficult. There are other methods that the criminals rely on, such as smuggling people and illegal drugs in vehicles, or digging elaborate tunnels that stretch from buildings located in Tijuana to buildings on the US side of the border. Although there is no single foolproof solution to the border issue, there is no question in my mind that the fence has significantly deterred illegal crossings and related activity in the San Diego border vicinity. However, the fence has an adverse impact on the more remote border areas. Criminals naturally flock to areas without a fence; much like what would happen if a dam was only completed halfway, the water would simply flow around the sides. The open sides beyond the border fence are in remote areas that can require hours of driving and hiking to access.

Understandably, mere mention of a border fence brings controversy and immediate comparisons to the Berlin Wall and Cold War oppression. The reality is that illegal aliens cross the border on foot in unfenced areas, only to be subjected to the harsh conditions of the desert. They frequently die of thirst, exposure, and heat exhaustion. A border fence certainly does not come close to fixing all current immigration issues, but it would have an immediate positive impact. Ultimately these fences have helped improved the safety of both US citizens and illegals by stemming the flow of foot traffic across the border. The United States is virtually powerless to combat the violence and drug related challenges in Mexico, but we can absolutely do a better job of protecting our own country by completing the fence along our southern border, and investing in the people and technology resources that are necessary to truly secure the border.

One evening my supervisor called me and said that an AFO had been reported, and that he had picked my squad mate, Special Agent Mark Landry, and me to handle the investigation. We convened at the FBI office and then drove out to a United States border patrol checkpoint southeast of San Diego, which took approximately one hour of driving on small winding roads to reach. By telephone we learned some rough details about the incident. An officer attempted to stop a vehicle at the checkpoint, was unsuccessful, and became tangled in the seatbelt of the vehicle as it pulled away. The officer was able to run alongside the car and free himself and escaped without injury; despite not being injured, the action of the criminals was technically an assault on the officer. A high-speed chase ensued from the checkpoint, ultimately ending with the subjects being arrested in Chula Vista, California. The Chula Vista Police Department successfully and safely stopped the vehicle, and the subjects were returned to the location of the checkpoint so the interviews and investigation could be conducted.

Mark and I made the lengthy drive to the checkpoint, and as I watched the desert landscape and mountains pass, I selfishly could only think of how late it would be before I was able to go home. I knew we would be arriving at the scene at about midnight, and that these investigations can take many hours to complete. The professional side of me knew that this was a serious investigation, but another part of me realized that nobody had been seriously injured, and I was somewhat resentful that people who were probably illegally in the country had turned my sleeping hours into waking hours.

We finally arrived at the checkpoint where the subjects were being detained. The scene was located on a two-lane highway that runs in the vicinity of the California and Mexico border. The checkpoint is in place to prevent people referred to as "coyotes" from picking up illegal aliens who cross the border, who are then taken into sanctuary cities, such as the San Diego suburb called National City, where the local law enforcement refuses to participate in enforcing federal immigration laws, and are essentially granted a free pass from being deported.

Through the course of the investigation we were granted access to view the videotape of the incident, and it was indeed a terrifying scene to witness. It reminded me of the late-night extreme shock videos on TV that do not always result in a safe outcome. Fortunately in this case the officer who was involved had no visible injuries, although he was clearly and understandably shaken up. After seeing the video, putting myself in the shoes of the agent who narrowly escaped with his life, I realized that the FBI really did need to be there to ensure that this case would be advanced and presented to the US Attorney's Office for prosecution. I knew that we needed to take a stance and not allow anyone to just waltz into our country and endanger the men and women who work so hard to protect legitimate and legal citizens.

We learned more about the subjects involved with the case; they were two Hispanic female US citizens who were in their late teens. They had picked up two illegal immigrants near the border and were attempting to drive them to a safe location in the United States. After reviewing their criminal histories, we found out that the two females had prior records of being arrested for illegal alien smuggling. They had managed to wriggle their way out of charges on eight previous occasions, which seemed to indicate not only a serious pattern of bad behavior on their part, but also serious failings on the part of our justice system. They had been set free and were allowed to commit the same crime a ninth time, when the result easily could have been the injury or death of a law enforcement official.

The other two occupants of the vehicle were from Mexico. They seemed scared and clearly they had just been along for the ride during the incident. They had probably paid thousands of dollars so that they could be taken into the United States, and instead were caught and would ultimately be deported back to Mexico. They had possibly given up their life savings and everything they had trying to make it into the United States, and this was the result. Although it is not the place of an FBI agent to judge, I felt my anger directed much more towards the girls than toward the illegals they were trying to smuggle into the United States.

Unfortunately the illegals did not speak English. My wonderful squad mate, Janet, who always amazed me with her positive and pleasant attitude, even when called in the middle of the night to assist, drove out to the scene so that she could translate and perform interviews of the Spanish-speaking illegals. I realized the significant resource drain on my squad from this one incident, and could mentally envision the number of incidents that I knew that frequently occur along the United States border. Prior to joining the FBI, I had never thought about the FBI having to expend resources to combat illegal immigration. That was Homeland Security's problem. In this case the FBI sent out three of only eight squad members to perform an investigation, which resulted in days of paperwork and follow-up action, meaning that several days of precious time were not be available for us to spend on other critical investigations such as bank robberies, fugitives, kidnappings, or extortions.

The scene of the incident was at the same checkpoint where everyone was being held for their interviews. At one point during the evening, I witnessed a Border Patrol car peeling out of the parking lot racing down the highway. I later saw ambulances and fire trucks coming down the same road, whizzing by the checkpoint at high speed. Word quickly spread that a van with approximately ten illegal immigrants had approached the checkpoint, had turned around, was noticed and pursued by the Border Patrol, and then took off with a high-speed chase ensuing. The driver lost control of the vehicle on a perilous curved section of the highway, and plunged down a ravine approximately one hundred feet. According to the responding officers, there were bodies and carnage everywhere. Clearly there were additional significant resources being drained from not only the Border Patrol, but also medical personnel.

During my time in San Diego I would hear about multiple additional incidents that were similar to this. Vehicles crammed with people that crash while trying to flee from law enforcement were not uncommon. These dramatic events would be a headline new story in most areas of the country, but along the border these horrible occurrences are hardly noticed by media outlets.

We conducted a lengthy interview of the subjects. The hours slowly ticked by. We finally concluded all of our investigative activities at about 2 a.m. and headed back to the office. I headed home to get a few hours of sleep, and upon my return to the office at 7 a.m., I learned that my fellow agent had stayed up at the office all night. He was trying to finish the paperwork so that the records would be immediately available for the United States Attorney's Office to file their case in federal court. This was just another example of the dedication that FBI agents exhibit.

That late night at the border patrol station showed me what I call the true "Wild Wild West." I immediately gained an appreciation for an incredibly difficult job in harsh and dangerous conditions that agents in the United States Border Patrol do on a daily basis. I could see that in the law-enforcement community my job was relatively safe, with clean conditions and a desirable location. And while I could not afford to buy a home in Southern California, I was well-paid relative to other law enforcement positions; while I had my share of justifiable complaints, I was certainly in an enviable position from the perspective of most law enforcement officers. This learning experience also helped me to conclude that the true cost of illegal immigration is incalculable. Actions by the dedicated individuals in law enforcement are not going to fix this problem; ultimately, it comes down to the leaders in Congress and the White House making the tough policy decisions that will address immigration issues head-on.

CHAPTER 35

Kidnappings

During my time in the San Diego FBI, we received an average of one reported kidnapping every one to two weeks. Out of about fifty kidnappings in the San Diego area that were reported to the FBI, all but two had at least some involvement or tie to victims, families, and subjects who were not US citizens. The two cases that involved only US citizens both had ties to illegal activities in Mexico. All cases pointed towards broader issues of our lack of immigration law enforcement and to a porous border. Not once while I was in San Diego did the FBI get a call that most people envision when they hear the term kidnapping. There were no little girls trapped in wells being held captive by psychotic killers. There were no *Silence of the Lambs* type of cases.

Kidnappings in San Diego tended to follow similar patterns, not unlike what we observed for bank robberies. Quite frequently at the end of the day on Friday, or possibly early on a Saturday morning, the FBI San Diego office would receive a call from a person saying that a relative had been kidnapped. The FBI rightfully prioritizes kidnappings over other investigations, because a life may be hanging in the balance; the FBI always places the safety and the welfare of citizens (and non-citizens) ahead of all other concerns. During my experience in the San Diego FBI office, I saw that the kidnapping problem is rampant, and that dozens of agents could be dedicated full-time to investigating kidnappings and still not have the resources needed to thoroughly pursue all leads and provide the type of response that most citizens assume the FBI will provide if they pick up the phone and report a kidnapping.

For every reported kidnapping while I was in San Diego, I estimate that another ten occurred which were never reported to authorities. The small percentage that are reported are usually not known to law enforcement until several days after the kidnapping occurs. The reason for these surprising figures is that family members who report the kidnapping are often profiting from illegal activities that their kidnapped family member is engaged in. Kidnappings in the San Diego vicinity were commonly related to drug dealing, typically with a specific debt to be collected as ransom money. This is often an oddly specific amount, such as $153,000, for example. An oddly specific amount alerts law enforcement that a drug debt is likely to be involved, since the ransom amount is not a "round" number, such as $100,000. At other times, ransom amounts would be for several million dollars, and much like the process of negotiating a leather purse in a Mexican market, a deal could be struck between a victim's family and kidnappers when the right amount of pressure was applied and kidnappers were convinced that the victim's financial resources were completely tapped. In some cases, I saw ransom demands negotiated down to as little as 10% of the original asking price. However, in those instances, the chances of getting back a kidnapping victim alive were even lower than 10%. Negotiating on the price seemed to have little impact on the chances of a safe return of the victim. The rampant kidnapping problems in the San Diego area highlighted the extreme reward and risk associated with the drug trade.

There were several additional complexities that impacted the kidnapping investigations that I was involved with. Victims typically carried unregistered cell phones sold in Mexico, family members were usually based in Mexico, and despite whether the victims or relatives were US citizens, the FBI was legally obligated to help them and pursue criminal charges whenever possible. While the FBI has no jurisdiction to perform an investigation in a foreign country, if telephone calls for ransom were made from Mexico to the United States, that triggered the legal mechanism within Title 18 of the United States code to pursue an investigation. Family members knew that FBI agents could be trusted, so when they became desperate enough, they would come to the United States for help because they did not trust their own law enforcement entities. In most cases, the FBI agents' hands were tied in pursuing a fruitful investigation since surveillance, cell phone tracking and monitoring, and other aspects of the investigation could physically only occur in Mexico, yet FBI agents generally were not allowed to enter Mexico to perform those tasks. Frequently the family who reports the kidnapping would specifically not want the FBI to report the kidnapping to the Mexican authorities, since the Mexican authorities were often corruptly tied in with the drug cartels. If a kidnapper instructed the family not to work with the police and word got back to the kidnappers that the family was working with the FBI, then the odds of successfully saving the victim became slimmer.

Not only were victim's family members frequently not US citizens, but they often could not even speak English. Translators had to be brought in, and communication was difficult. When interviewing relatives of kidnap victims, I often witnessed a sudden onset degree of deafness or lack of understanding of the translator; this conveniently would occur when they were asked questions such as "Is the victim involved in the illegal drug trade?" or "Are you involved in the illegal drug trade?"

Criminals are aware of the limitations placed on law enforcement from an international perspective. Criminals use the border to their advantage by hopping back and forth between the United States and Mexico so they can evade law enforcement on both sides. There are tens of thousands of people and cars travelling between the two countries on a daily basis. The ability to stop illegal activity appears to be a losing game. The best criminal deterrent that the United States has is to build an effective barrier or fence and embrace technology to help verify the legal status of those who are travelling between the two countries, including facial recognition, fingerprints, and eventually DNA analysis. While I see this as more government intrusion (which I am generally opposed to), failure to do more to secure the border eventually will lead to failure of the country.

Another unexpected and despicable occurrence that I observed was a kidnapping scenario unfolding in which multiple parties would independently contact the victim's family with ransom demands. Unless the kidnappers were willing to provide some type of proof of life, there would be no way to know who the "real" kidnappers were, versus other parties who had simply heard about the kidnapping and were attempting to make a profit. That disgusted me even more than did the genuine kidnappers; I had never imagined how low people would stoop to make "easy" money.

While each case was different, one area that consistently provided difficulty throughout each kidnapping ordeal was managing the family members' expectations. If a random person on the street is polled, "What happens when a kidnapping gets reported to the FBI?", he or she would likely respond, "The FBI swoops in with high-tech devices, helicopters, and teams of people in both suits and tactical gear who are standing by 24/7 to rescue kidnapping victims." In a world that has further evolved even beyond the forensic brilliance shown in *Silence of the Lambs*, most citizens think that with a cotton swab, a chemical test, and with some fingerprinting, a high-tech computer network can somehow provide an immediate answer on the location of a victim and the identify of a kidnapper. Surely the hardest part for the FBI is just getting a recovery team down in a well, or hiking to a remote cabin to save a helpless little girl from "the bad guy." The fact that the FBI has absolutely no jurisdiction in Mexico amazes the families of kidnapping victims; they are shocked that the FBI cannot subpoena phone records, monitor phone calls, or perform any law enforcement duties in Mexico. This also puzzles victims of other crimes that occur in Mexico but are reported to US authorities; in 95% of these cases, there is nothing the FBI can do to help. Mexico is a completely separate country. It is not a state within the US, although many kidnapping victim's families truly seemed not to grasp that concept; some families appeared to think of the border as nothing more significant than a toll booth on the highway.

Another common misconception is that the FBI has a stash of ransom money available to give to kidnappers. That is not the case. If a family member can only come up with $100 for a $100,000 ransom, the FBI will not pay the difference. The FBI does have access to marked bills that can be exchanged with ransom money provided by the victim's families, but that is the limit of the help the FBI can offer related to ransom money, even if it is likely the money will be recovered. Ultimately, the choice to pay a ransom demand comes down to the family. The FBI will not decide that for the family, and the FBI's level of involvement is largely left up to the family. If the family wants to pay a ransom with no FBI involvement, they are free to do so. Of course the FBI wants to be involved so that the criminals can be caught, but this sometimes conflicts with the notion that family members often have that the best odds of getting their loved one back is to have the FBI out of the picture.

Part of the standard protocol when working a kidnapping investigation is to obtain criminal background checks on everybody who is associated with a kidnapping, including the victim and the victim's family members. Once the victim's criminal history is obtained, the FBI has an indicator of the type of trouble that the victim may be in. Frequently, a victim will have a lengthy criminal history, with drug related activity. But regardless of criminal history, the FBI treats every kidnapping with the same sense of urgency, and everyone gets the same treatment. In San Diego, the FBI agents who worked kidnappings operated independently from the drug investigations squad; even if the kidnapping victim is rescued but believed to be involved with drug trafficking, the FBI is only concerned with the safety and recovery of the victim. Any intelligence or evidence obtained during the course of a kidnapping investigation can legally be used against the kidnappers or kidnap victim by prosecutors, but most of my experience with kidnappings was focused solely on the victim and victim's family members.

During the process of working kidnappings with criminal elements in the United States that the FBI could actively pursue, I learned about the difficulties for FBI agents to obtain any form of electronic surveillance, including the tactical and legal ability to listen in on phone conversations and to see where phone calls are originating from and going to. Even obtaining a subscriber's name for a cell phone number required a subpoena from a court, which proved to be a cumbersome and difficult process to navigate, especially when the need usually surfaced during weekend or evening hours. I found myself often turning to database searches, including public "Google" searches, which provided the fastest response and often the best information available. In direct contrast to the public's perception, the FBI does not have any magical data or information pipeline to obtain citizens' personal information based on a phone number. There are some basic tools such as the indexed information found in the FBI's files, but this information is primarily based on interviews and outdated written reports. The FBI also has access to credit bureau information, but this is a far cry from what most people would expect. The FBI has to go through the appropriate legal mechanisms to obtain information; the FBI does not flip a magical switch and start listening to the "bad guys." The difficulty in obtaining electronic information reaches nearly impossible levels for criminal activity in Mexico. As a result, the FBI would sometimes provide tape recorders to kidnap victims' families with the instruction to record the kidnappers if they called. This was an embarrassing solution that would have seemed outdated twenty years ago, and in today's electronic world this seemed to be about as helpful as telling someone to bring a pocketknife to a gunfight. The FBI agents who fight traditional crime are often fighting with their hands tied behind their backs.

On one occasion a white female in her early 20s had gone missing in Mexico, and her father contacted the FBI for help. There had been a call placed from Mexico to him in which the caller had hung up without speaking, and he was greatly concerned about her safety and was convinced that she been kidnapped. Serving as the case agent, I immediately began the process of working the telephone company to begin tracking incoming and outgoing telephone numbers for the victim's cell phone. Minutes can make a difference early on with a kidnapping investigation, and I wanted to do everything I could to help. I had yet to see a kidnapping situation in which the victim was completely innocent and not tied in with criminal activity, but this case had the opportunity to be the first. In addition, I really felt bad for the father, who was as worried as a parent can be about the safety of his child. In an emergency situation like this one, a telephone company legally must work with the FBI to provide information with the agreement that a court order authorizing the activity will be provided within a twenty-four hour period. I began to work with the United States Attorney's Office to get the appropriate paperwork, a court order. As the minutes passed, other agents who were assisting me began doing a background check on the victim and learned that the victim was currently residing at a rehabilitation center somewhere on the coast in central California. The strong possibility began to sink in that the victim had just walked out of rehab and simply headed down to Tijuana for drugs.

My intuition was right. A couple of hours after the entire incident had begun, the father received a telephone call from his daughter saying that she was fine and that she had just gone down to Tijuana for "fun" and was driving back up to the Los Angeles area. The father was appreciative for the FBI's assistance, and was embarrassed and sorry for the trouble he had caused. Indeed, he and his daughter had created more legal trouble for the FBI than I could have imagined. We had begged the phone company to provide sensitive information for one of their customers with the promise of a court order for an emergency situation. The phone company provided phone records, but with the promise of swiftly receiving a court order authorizing them to do so. While the emergency situation had gone away, the phone company's requirement to receive a court order had not. Unfortunately, the federal judge who was to provide the court order passed word back to us that he could not issue the court order in good faith since the facts of the case had changed and since there was no longer a question about the victim's immediate safety. The problem was that the phone company was understandably sensitive about this type of action since there were frequent headlines in the media about telephone companies doing illegal activities and spying on customers without court orders, sensationalized headlines that continue to dominate the news cycle when there are no other major stories to follow. While the details of this event should have been straightforward to even the most suspicious conspiracy theorists, a headline of "Phone Company Continues to Provide Customer Information Illegally" could have easily become a reality.

This particular issue for my case was escalated to the highest management levels in the FBI San Diego Division, and for several days following this kidnapping incident I had to provide numerous records and documentation that explained why we had obtained information from a telephone company and why we were not going to be able to get a court order to legally authorized this activity. Being a process-oriented person, I immediately saw that there was a flaw in the overall process for obtaining the court order. No individuals throughout the process had acted incorrectly, yet the end result was not satisfactory. To remedy the situation, I drafted a letter to the telephone company, and our Special Agent in Charge of the San Diego Division personally signed and sent the letter. Although this document was not a court order, it did explain that the FBI had done everything within its power to obtain a court order, but that the judge was simply unable to provide this since the facts of the case had changed. In summary, a simple event of a kidnapping false alarm chewed up a number of hours for valuable FBI resources, created work for US Attorney's Office, and wasted the time of a federal judge.

I found myself again seeing that the reality of being an FBI agent did not at all match up with my expectations. The majority of my time as an agent was spent trying to navigate a complex process of paperwork and legal requirements that was not only stressful, but also impeded my ability to do my job effectively. The concerns that people have of the FBI abusing its power now seem almost ridiculous. The FBI is made of responsible agents who follow the law and are in the profession for the right reasons, and the paranoid thought that many share of agents having time to sit around and listen in on routine conversations of citizens without reason is absolutely preposterous. If the general public knew how much the FBI's powers are limited and how thin resources are spread, there would be much less fear about overreach and abuse by the FBI.

CHAPTER 36

Expect the Unexpected

My squad, a catch-all squad known for pursuing violent criminals and major offenders, had a reputation for not being afraid to roll up our sleeves and get our hands dirty. As a result, San Diego VCMO (Violent Crimes and Major Offenders) agents were often the first to lead the charge to resolve whatever urgent issue might arise at the FBI office. One morning I was sitting at my desk, sipping my coffee, and working on some paperwork when I heard a page from the overhead speakers for "anyone to pick up on Squad 11." Squad 11 was my squad. That usually meant serious trouble had arisen, such as a kidnapping, a bank robbery, or an assault on a federal officer. But this case was different; after picking up the phone and talking to our operator, I discovered that immediate help was needed to arrest somebody who was physically in the building. This day was certainly not shaping up to be like a normal day in my old corporate job. In the FBI, I truly could "expect the unexpected."

As a standard operating protocol, the FBI does a high-level background check on every person allowed into an FBI facility. The San Diego office was undergoing a remodeling project which employed several contracted workers. These workers were subject to the same check that anyone else is subject to when entering the closely guarded grounds of the FBI. One of the workers had an outstanding arrest warrant issued by the State of California for a non-violent crime. Regardless of the nature of the arrest warrant, anyone who is wanted by law enforcement should be considered dangerous. Fortunately, the background check was done while the subject waited in the lobby; however, we knew we had to act quickly to ensure the safety of the office and any visitors in the greeting area.

We located and approached the worker and asked him if we could speak to him privately. He made no sudden moves and was cooperative. In a side hallway, we informed him that he was under arrest, and I asked him to turn around and place his hands behind his back. After handcuffing the worker, we escorted him down to an interview room, and proceeded to ask him questions about his warrant. The man told us that he was unaware that a warrant was outstanding for his arrest, but that he knew he had some problems related to a bitter divorce and custody battle. We continued to talk with the subject until the San Diego PD squad car arrived, and then we transferred custody of the prisoner so that local law enforcement officials could pursue the State of California charges.

After the arrest I headed back up to my squad area and was greeted by a small crowd. They excitedly peppered me with questions. Not unlike many corporate environments, at the FBI, the vast majority of employees work normal business hours in a cube, and are rarely exposed to actual arrest scenarios. For someone to be arrested in the FBI building was a memorable event for the office, even if the subject was completely cooperative and non-violent.

My squad handled a disproportionate amount of activity and arrests compared to other areas within the office, such as the white collar and terrorism areas, which tended to have lengthy and proactive investigations. While I would have greatly preferred to be on one of the squads that have more predictable days and more complex investigations, I also felt a great sense of pride to be combatting violent crime for the FBI, which was a highly respected area of expertise within the ranks of the agents.

CHAPTER 37

Top Ten Fugitive

The FBI is well known for the top ten "Most Wanted" criminal list publicized nationwide and seen in police stations, post offices, and government buildings throughout the United States. The list is something of an "all-star" reference to the most heinous wanted criminals in the world. During my time in San Diego, the list was topped by Osama bin Laden (referred to by the FBI as "Usama," which is a technically correct Romanization of bin Laden's first name), with the remaining positions occupied by violent gangsters and murderers. While I had pursued leads and tips on the location of fugitives, each with a predictably low probability of successfully locating any of the top ten criminals, there was one occasion on which the FBI office believed with near certainty that one of these horrible criminals had indeed been found.

Robert William Fisher, a former fireman in Scottsdale, Arizona, was the tenth person on the most wanted list. He had intentionally burned up his house with his family inside. This arsonist and murderer was believed to have fled to Mexico. He was known to possess high powered weapons and was considered to be extremely dangerous. This guy was the worst of the worst.

The San Diego office received a call from a Mexican law enforcement official claiming to have located and arrested Robert William Fisher. Fisher had supposedly admitted to being a top ten fugitive, and every indicator showed that this was a positive match. No fingerprint or DNA tests had been performed, but a visual match, including physical characteristics and identifying marks, aligned with known information about the subject.

Word spread quickly, creating an intense level of excitement and buzz within the FBI office. If indeed the actual fugitive had been captured and was being returned to the United States, his capture would generate massive national media interest. However, prior to the FBI contacting the media, we wanted to be absolutely certain that he was the right man. Since my squad worked fugitive violations, two squad mates and I were assigned the task of validating the identify of this person and taking custody of him from the Mexican authorities. With lights flashing we rushed down to the San Ysidro border crossing to take custody of the prisoner. Coordination between US and Mexican law enforcement is notoriously difficult; we did not want to be late and risk having this top ten fugitive slip between our fingers.

After waiting in the "no-man's land" vicinity between the US and Mexican entry points, we finally caught sight of a well-built man in handcuffs being led by Mexican authorities. As a true gesture of cooperation, with few words and little fanfare the Mexican officials simply turned him over to us, and then turned around and marched back into Mexico. With some attitude and a smirk, I told the subject, "Welcome back to the United States." But this was no joking matter; this man had reportedly killed his family members and burned them. As a former firefighter and trusted member of the public safety community, his crime was an atrocity that is rare even in our largely imperfect society

The subject immediately launched into a lengthy plea about how he was not the person we were looking for, which seemed like something that any top ten fugitive would say in a last desperate attempt to elude law enforcement. We ignored him and led him to a secured location within the US border crossing offices. We began the process of obtaining fingerprints from the subject, and helpful Border Patrol officials helped us with the process of matching fingerprints to the AFIS (Automated Fingerprint Information System) database that is managed by the FBI and utilized by law enforcement entities around the United States.

While we were waiting for fingerprint results that would provide the final official confirmation of our top ten fugitive's identity, the subject became increasingly difficult to speak with. Other agents were making him mad, and while visually he appeared to be the correct subject, I could see the frustration building on both sides. I escorted him into a holding room where I sat with him for some time and continued to speak with him with the hope of getting his cooperation in either confirming that he was the fugitive, or revealing his true identity if he was not Fisher. When I was able to speak with him one-on-one, he began to calm down and told me what he claimed to be his real name, which was not Robert Fisher, the name of the top ten fugitive. At that point I still believed that he was a cold-blooded killer, and I personally did not feel like humoring him. But I knew that the FBI was waiting to make a major announcement to the media, and that we needed to have zero doubt about his identity. It was time to put a smile on my face and continue to talk to this person as if he were a rational human being. The more I talked to him, the more likely we could quickly determine his true identity, which could later be confirmed by his fingerprints.

I calmed him down by saying that he did not have to worry about a mistaken identity; the FBI would figure that part out. Although he was uncooperative initially, he finally began to provide the details to support his claimed identity, including his name, date of birth, and social security number. I relayed that information to other agents, who called back to the San Diego office to check on that identity. Even if the information pertained to a real person, it could be a case of stolen identity. This criminal had evaded law enforcement for years, so I was not about to let my guard down.

As I awaited word back on the confirmation of identity, I

continued to talk to the subject and listen to his story. He had enough details to share that I began to wonder if he was the criminal we believed him to be. We began to talk about other random subjects, including music and sports. He said he was a former BMX champion in Southern California, and I truthfully told him that I was a former motocross racer, although my novice level skills were about as far from a champion as anyone can get. His face immediately lit up and he explained that his family was the former owner and operator of the premier motocross track in California called Glen Helen. I told him that only a few months earlier I had been to the track to watch the outdoor motocross national race. He thought that it was amazing that an FBI agent would share interests and a background similar to his own, and his attitude shifted from confrontational to collaborative. While I was still unsure of his identity, I played the part of the laid back agent that he could talk to like any regular guy on the street. The topic shifted to music, and he mentioned a quote by Dee Snyder, which almost felt like a test to see if I was really the "ordinary dude" that he could talk to freely, or if I was an FBI agent trying to lure him into a false sense of security. I immediately continued the conversation and informed him that the 80s hair band "Twisted Sister" was one of my favorites, and that Dee Snyder was an underrated rock genius. We even talked about some of the band's best songs, and mutually agreed that while the band was considered to be something of a one-album-hit wonder, they really were underappreciated and their music will stand the test of time. By this point he was really starting to relax, which told me that he probably was not the fugitive we were looking for. We chatted a bit longer, and I genuinely assured him that once we could confirm his true identity he would be released with an apology and would be free to go. He even agreed that he understood that mistaken identities happen, and said that he could see that the FBI must pursue top ten fugitive leads aggressively for the public good.

The results came back from the fingerprint comparison,

which proved that he was not the criminal we had believed him to be. His true identity was confirmed, and we verified that he was not wanted for any crimes. He was incredibly relieved when he learned that we no longer believed he was the fugitive. Since he had calmed down and had reached an amazingly friendly status with me, I asked why in the world he would ever tell the Mexican authorities that he was a top ten fugitive. He denied saying that, and insisted that people had peppered him with questions in Spanish, and that he had not known what he was being arrested for until he was in our custody. I did not know if his claim was completely true. One sarcastic remark such as "Yeah, right!" could have been misconstrued as an admission of guilt.

We walked him out of the building, and after a complicated "cool guy" style handshake and "great talking with you, bro" comment to me, he disappeared into the throngs of people passing between the two countries on foot. A couple of agents chuckled and could not believe how I had managed to befriend this person who initially had been incredibly angry and difficult to deal with. We were all thankful that the media had not yet been alerted about nabbing a most wanted fugitive, which would have been embarrassing for the FBI, since we had the wrong man. This was par for the course in hunting fugitives. Robert Fisher remained on the FBI's Most Wanted list. Although we did not find the real fugitive, I enjoyed the overall experience. I was able to use my strength of being able to talk to people and find common ground which would continue to serve me well in the FBI while interviewing witnesses or interrogating subjects. The skill of conversation, which in the FBI can lead to admission of guilt, is truly one of the most powerful weapons in an FBI agent's arsenal.

CHAPTER 38

Interrogation

One quiet morning I was sitting at my desk when a call came in about a suspect who had been arrested by the San Diego Police Department. He was believed to be a bank robber, and was possibly involved with a string of McDonald's restaurant robberies that had occurred over the last few weeks. I made a dash for my car to head to the downtown SDPD headquarters, where the suspect was being held. After a quick journey downtown, I parked and strolled into the main SDPD prisoner intake and receiving area, located in the basement of the building.

The subject was restrained by handcuffs and was attached to a chair. He was sitting out in the open, which was unusual since suspects are typically placed in a cell or guarded in an interview room. This subject had spit on police officers who had arrested him; his head was in a mesh hood, similar to what a beekeeper uses, to prevent him from spitting on others. Approximately one dozen police officers were eyeing me because I was designated as case agent and was representing the FBI; my presence had the attention of everyone in the vicinity. My objective was to interrogate the subject and get a confession, and I could feel the pressure of having an audience of seasoned police veterans watching. Not only was my personal pride on the line, but the FBI's image and reputation was also at stake, at least to a small degree. As I looked around the room and mentally prepared for my performance, I did my best to convey a sense of confidence and control that people expect the FBI to bring to any given situation.

I sat in a chair across from the handcuffed subject and began to question him. I spoke with the subject directly, and told him, "I am an FBI agent, and I will be straight with you. I would like to speak with you and hear your side of the story, and I would prefer to have a normal conversation where you are not wearing a hood." The subject agreed to behave, and I felt that the quality of information I could obtain with a more relaxed prisoner outweighed the risk of being spit on.

After removing the hood, I continued to employ the FBI techniques I had learned to help get information from difficult people. I confronted him with the evidence that was found, including clothing, and told him we had a positive identification through surveillance video. I told him that there was nothing that he could do to help his case except to cooperate, and that I would make a note of his level of cooperation in my report and pass that information along to prosecutors. Unlike some depictions on TV, FBI agents do not have the ability to make deals to get information. However, they can imply that they will try to help out the person who is being questioned, even though the reality is that if a person confesses, little to no weight will be given towards the level of cooperation that the subject showed after being arrested.

After about twenty minutes of my speaking with the subject, he confessed by rambling about how his "imaginary friend" made him do the robbery. With excellent witness identification and robbery video footage, there was really no question about whether he had committed the bank robbery. However, this confession was the icing on the prosecutorial cake and would almost guarantee that the criminal would face stiff penalties for his actions. In addition, I knew that the confession could help all parties avoid the entire trial process, since a confessed criminal is more likely to take almost any deal that the AUSA (for federal cases) or DA (for state cases) can offer that will help him avoid the absolute maximum penalty for his crime. I was proud to have this result, especially while representing the FBI and being watched by a large crowd of local police officers.

But despite the bank robbery confession, my work was not complete; the San Diego PD also suspected that the subject could be linked to a series of McDonald's restaurant robberies. Although a fast food restaurant robbery was not a federal crime and not generally an FBI matter, if I could also get a confession to those crimes, that could be legally used against the subject. Before the interview, I had been provided a summary of the robberies, and I knew that there was not solid evidence to link this person to the McDonald's robberies. It was time to put on my poker face and see if I could bluff my way to a confession. The pressure was on.

I shifted my focus, and decided to directly tell the subject, "We know what you did; things will go easier for you if you'll just admit to the McDonald's robberies." His demeanor instantly changed from pretending to have imaginary friends and making wild statements to suddenly becoming very serious, and he was absolutely insistent that he "most certainly hadn't robbed no McDonald's." When it came down to being blamed for a crime he did not commit, his mind morphed into a coherent state, and he adamantly denied any knowledge of the McDonald's bank robberies.

While I know that criminals are commonly liars and will try to talk their way out of anything, in this case I believed that the subject truly had no involvement with the McDonald's robberies. If he did, then he deserved an Academy Award for his acting ability. I felt that my work was done, so I concluded the interview, and the police took him back to a holding cell. I was able to walk out of the interview knowing that I had done my job and represented the FBI well in front of our law enforcement partners.

CHAPTER 39

Red Wire or Blue?

On a warm day early in the summer of 2007, Jennifer and I were getting ready to take a long weekend trip through the Southwest. I had worked every single week and weekend for the previous two months, and we were anxious to get away and enjoy some non-FBI quality time together. The continuous action and stress in my job was quickly burning me out, and I was very much looking forward to this break.

Just a couple of hours before we planned to head out on our trip, the FBI received a bank robbery alarm notification, and I was the first available resource to respond. I arrived at the bank robbery scene and learned that a subject had already been caught by the San Diego Sheriff's Department. The most time consuming aspect of an investigation comes after a subject is caught; of course, we wanted to get criminals off the street, but we knew that a pile of paperwork followed every arrest, with a window measured in hours to get everything in order to enable a successful prosecution. Since I was first to respond, by default I became the case agent for this bank robbery, and I would be responsible for a number of steps in the legal process chain for the coming days and weeks. My heart sank and I felt a great deal of disappointment, knowing that I might not be able to take my weekend trip. While that may sound selfish, the repeated working weekends had me at my mental limit. Frankly, I was sick of the job at this point, and because of the dangers posed, Jennifer was also not a fan of the profession. Regular hours of working on a sanitation truck sounded more appealing than the crazy life of an FBI agent working violent crime.

But I was fortunate to be a part of an extremely hard-working group of FBI agents. A squad mate agreed to take over the case, type up the necessary paperwork, and tie up loose ends so I could get out of town. This sharing of the workload by FBI agents helped to make the job tolerable and was appreciated immensely. I only had to finish interrogating the subject and process evidence taken from the scene of the bank robbery that was being held at the local San Diego Sheriff's Department substation.

The majority of the bank robberies in the San Diego vicinity fall within the city limits and are within the jurisdiction of the knowledgeable and experienced San Diego Police Department. However, this particular robbery was in the neighboring community of Lemon Grove, which meant that I would have less experienced deputies to work with, although the vast majority of those officers had much more law enforcement experience than I did.

I arrived at the robbery scene and walked into a stressful, complex, and taxing environment. I was immediately bombarded with multiple deputies asking what they should be doing. I quickly was unofficially looked on as the leader of this law enforcement frenzy; I performed my duties responsibly; but I did not welcome the tasks at hand. I directed the deputies to conduct interviews, to obtain fingerprints, and to work with the bank to obtain video evidence. The FBI could later use this evidence as needed, depending on whether the prosecution was heading towards a state or federal route. I personally interviewed some of the key witnesses and ensured that fellow agents were able to assist with wrapping everything up at the bank.

Before I could head home and load up the car for a road trip, I had one last task to accomplish. The robber had taken cash from the bank teller and placed it in a brown paper bag. A device called a dye pack was concealed within the middle of a stack of cash, which would be handed to a robber in the case of a bank robbery. Dye packs are designed to explode when they leave the vicinity of the bank. They leave a bright colored dye substance that that makes it easy for law enforcement to identify and capture robbery subjects. In this case, the subject had taken one of the stacks of cash with a dye pack, but for unknown reasons the electronics had failed and the dye pack was still active but had not exploded.

Dye packs had a bad reputation for exploding at unexpected times. My supervisor had previously told me a story about hauling evidence back to the FBI office after a bank robbery, and suddenly having a dye pack detonate inside his car. The dye pack had enough force to rip open a water jug in his car, and had created a colorful mess in his vehicle. Knowledge of this event seemed to foreshadow an afternoon of possibly building memories that would be passed down through the FBI ranks like a watch gets handed down from fathers to sons.

To my dismay, the deputies at the sheriff's station did not have knowledge of how to disarm the device. They had the paper bag with the money placed in a jail cell, which they figured was safe until the FBI would show up and handle it. I was the lucky FBI agent tasked with the tackling this problem. The only problem was that I had no idea what to do. I immediately got on the phone with a seasoned San Diego Police Department detective who had worked countless bank robberies. I knew that he was my best shot at finding someone to tell me how to defuse this device.

The SDPD detective was a true professional and expert; he told me he could walk me through how to disable the device. He warned me of something I already knew: it could go off at any second, possibly causing minor injury and major embarrassment to me. Absolute worst case, I thought I might lose a couple of fingers and a suit. One of the female deputies was concerned about my eyes, so I borrowed her "blade" style sunglasses for the task at hand. Armed with a pocketknife and a cell phone with a SDPD detective on the line, I entered the jail cell containing the paper bag. I approached the bag, and turned around to a view of an extraordinary number of faces packed around the perimeter of the cell. The deputies seemed to be really enjoying watching a good show. While this was a far cry from an actual bomb, at that moment I felt like I was Bruce Willis in a *Die Hard* movie, and I halfway expected there to be a red wire and blue wire, and I would have to flip a coin to figure out which one to cut.

The SDPD detective on the phone began to walk me through the steps to disarm the dye pack. I removed the cash from the bag and slowly cut away the money wrapper that only had the appearance of holding together the stack of bills that was concealing the dye-pack. Next, I peeled back the top layer of bills, and carefully moved a spring-loaded latch that reminded me of a mousetrap. Finally, I found two sets of wires that connected to the battery. I cut one of the wires (which happened to be black), and successfully disarmed the device. The deputies all applauded, and we all laughed with relief at the situation. I felt a bit silly for taking the task so seriously, and could only imagine the stress and nerves that our military members must endure when responding to a real bomb threat or removing unexploded ordinance.

On any given day an FBI agent may be called on to perform duties that he or she has never been trained to do. Agents must be flexible and able to quickly adapt. Sometimes this involves life or death situations. Despite not enjoying these moments as they occurred, I do enjoy these incidents in retrospect. I like to remember the unusual challenges that the job entailed and the impressive people whom I had the pleasure of knowing and working with along the way.

CHAPTER 40

Surveillance

During my training at the FBI Academy, my favorite operational training activity was our surveillance exercises. A team of FBI agents in different cars with radios followed people who were trying to elude us, and worked in tandem with unexpected participants that seemed straight out of a spy novel or movie. Fanning out on the local highways in towns in Northern Virginia was a true joy and a great learning experience. Unfortunately, our packed training schedule only allowed for a few surveillance practicals. However, much to my delight, I found out shortly after arriving in San Diego that surveillance would be one of the major activities that I would spend my time on in the field. This lived up to my expectation as being the most pleasurable activity I participated in while serving as an agent in the field. But surveillance is far from being enjoyable every minute. It can be tedious and boring, especially if an agent gets the feeling that he or she is wasting time and that the efforts will not yield fruitful results.

One of my earliest surveillance experiences in San Diego was observing an apartment of a woman believed to be associated with a violent fugitive who was wanted in Minnesota. I was alone in my car during several days and evenings, keeping an eye on the property, without a hint of the subject showing up. It did not take long for me to realize how much I stuck out like a sore thumb in the area, which was in the working class suburb of Santee. While I was dressed casually, my clothing was obviously something that would be more likely to be worn by an off-duty cop rather than a "boy from the hood." Making things worse, I had no other options than to use my FBI issued four-door Buick, which could only have been more blatant if the plates had said "US GVT." There was even an occasion on which a group of several children started riding their bicycles in circles around my car, until one worked up the bravery to approach my window and ask what I was doing. If I could have been filmed, the result would be a perfect instructional video on how to not conduct surveillance; this also would have made for an appropriate YouTube "fail" video. After a few days, I was pulled to other priorities and assignments, and other agents and I decided to play our hand and interview the former girlfriend of the fugitive. We followed her to her job, which was at casino located at a nearby Indian reservation. She was genuinely horrified that we would think she would still associate with her ex-boyfriend, and assured us she had not seen him for years. We thanked her for her time, and did not let her know that her apartment had been watched for several days. The fugitive was later captured in another state.

Another surveillance operation that I participated in was one that involved going to a hospital where the subject had a doctor's appointment. We decided that this was an excellent arrest scenario since the subject, a female from Thailand, would most likely be unarmed for her visit. Also, she would be presumably out of her element, which would be to our advantage when arresting her.

A team of several agents were told through an informant about the subject and the doctor's appointment. We set up surveillance on her house and followed her for about ten miles along the California freeways to her appointment. We had contacted other agents to assist with the arrest at the hospital, and by the time we reached her destination, the hospital parking lot was already crawling with agents. Our biggest worry was that she would spot agents and realize she was about to be arrested, but our agents successfully blended right in with the normal flow of patients at the busy facility.

We allowed her to go to her appointment, and decided to simply wait for her to come out and arrest her as she walked back to her vehicle. As the minutes passed, anticipation of the arrest built. I had "the eye" and was watching the hospital entrance, waiting for the subject. I saw her, identified her, and notified all agents that the subject had exited the building and was heading back to her car. As she reached her car, swarms of agents surprised her both on foot and by pulling up in vehicles with lights blazing. The reaction of the people in the parking lot was priceless; I am certain that most of them probably will never forget the day that they were simply going to doctor's appointment and then saw a multitude of FBI agents making an arrest. This particular scenario was fun since the action moved fast and the odds of a safe arrest were in our favor.

On another occasion, the FBI received information from an informant on the location of a suspected bank robber. The location was in a rough area near central San Diego, right off an I-15 exit. The informant turned out to be a former spouse of the subject, one who was engaged in a custody battle. The FBI frequently would obtain information from unhappy or disgruntled girlfriends, spouses, or friends of suspects.

I took up a position outside of the subject's house and waited. After a couple of hours, I saw movement through my binoculars, and I could see that it was indeed the subject we were looking for. The man finally walked to his car, got in, and drove away. He drove right past me, and I radioed back to all San Diego PD and FBI units that the subject was "rolling," which initiated the ensuing arrest.

The model typically used for a joint operation between the FBI and San Diego police was for the San Diego PD to do what officers call a "hot stop." This means that a normal black and white patrol unit would pull an arrest subject over in a low-key manner that would suggest a routine traffic stop. This helped to keep the arrest scenario from escalating and resulted in safer arrests. Although uniformed officers did the heavy lifting, they were usually more than anxious to participate and have the opportunity to arrest wanted criminals. And despite the tough talk that comes from many agents, the FBI is more than happy to pass along the risk and danger of arresting criminals to the local authorities when possible. Vehicle arrests in particular are considered to be extremely dangerous by the law enforcement community. Most shootouts and violent encounters tend to occur with vehicle arrest scenarios since the subjects often feel they have a chance to escape.

So for this particular arrest, a San Diego PD unit pulled over the subject. I was only about a half block away and could see that the arrest was going smoothly and without incident. Once the subject was secured, I drove up to assist. The subject was still wearing the shirt with a business logo reflecting where he worked. This did make me feel some sympathy for the subject, because the bank robbery had occurred a couple of years ago, and obviously the robber was working at a legitimate job and trying to make an honest living. He had made a poor choice at the age of eighteen, and now at the age of twenty would be facing a felony conviction with prison time for what was probably a one-time event.

This was a good lesson for anyone who thought he could get away with a bank robbery. The statute of limitations for bank robberies is only five years, which I found fascinating. Anyone could rob a bank and five years later write a book about his or her experience and not be subject to arrest. However, the government can seize the robber's assets for an indefinite period of time, so even fifty years after a bank robbery, the offender could become broke, even if his or her money was not directly "earned" from bank robberies. Still, I could not help but hypothesize about a scenario of robbing banks, setting up accounts overseas, and then returning to the United States five years after the last robbery to do interviews, book deals, and movie deals. I would not be surprised to see someone perform this dangerous form of a stunt in society's current reality show era.

On another bank robbery occasion, I took part in another

arrest of a subject who was arrested while driving his vehicle. This particular arrest occurred on a road alongside harbor that is adjacent to the San Diego airport. I was doing surveillance on the subject and radioing out information to San Diego PD. I identified the vehicle and watched the black and whites move in. Several units surrounded the subject, and I hopped out of my car with gun drawn. Once again I was appreciative of the police officers who were assuming almost all of the risk and danger associated with the arrest. If there was a problem, I would be safely tucked away behind my car door while they were exposed.

While watching the action of the arrest unfold, I suddenly noticed an elderly man standing upright directly next to me. He had decided to get out of his car and stroll up to me, even though I was crouched behind a car door with my gun drawn. He started to say something along the lines of "What's going on?" but I abruptly interrupted him mid-sentence and ordered him to get back in his car. I was lucky that no violence broke out, because he easily could have been hurt or killed. I learned that agents can never assume that people will exercise common sense. Apparently a scene with law enforcement officials with guns drawn while hiding behind their car doors is not enough of a signal for some people to clear the area. With a typical arrest scenario, there will be one or more law enforcement people who control the crowd and prevent unwanted access to crime or arrest scenes. Aside from the public safety dangers, this also helps keep agents and police officers safe from an ambush while their attention is focused on only one direction. But with many fast-developing arrest scenes, agents do not have the luxury of having dedicated traffic control personnel, and this was one of those situations.

A few weeks later, I encountered a similar arrest scenario. A bank robber had been identified by a witness as possibly living in an inexpensive hotel near Balboa Park in San Diego. The FBI and San Diego PD set up our surveillance, identified the subject, and watched him catch a cab. Typically, surveillance takes hours or even days to be productive, but we were fortunate enough to spot him within minutes of setting up our positions. The subject hailed a cab, and our radios erupted with communications on how the arrest should be performed. Following our usual protocol, the FBI deferred to the San Diego PD, who elected to pull over the taxi using marked units to perform the arrest. We had a caravan of various surveillance units following the cab on parallel streets, and my pulse quickened as I listed to the radio chatter with the marked SDPD units. Although the PD had two units for the arrest, both would pull the cab over from behind on a one-way street. Help was needed to block off the end of the street in case the subject fled, so a squad mate and I frantically raced ahead on side streets to get one block ahead of the spot where we anticipated the arrest would occur. The street was empty, and we could see the cab followed by the PD units with lights and sirens blazing, heading our direction. We knew this was a dangerous scenario because the robber had been armed during his bank robberies, and we did not want to jeopardize the life of a cab driver. However, he was likely heading to Mexico; this was a common practice for criminals in the San Diego vicinity. If he made it to Mexico, we might not ever locate him again, and we knew the Mexican government would do nothing to help arrest him. We did not want to risk his escaping and potentially doing more robberies, each with an elevated possibility of injury or death, since he was known to carry a weapon.

The cab driver pulled over, and the SDPD officers quickly swarmed in with guns drawn. The suspect did not put up a fight and was arrested without incident. My partner and I were able to watch from a safe distance, and felt lucky that the subject had not attempted to flee on foot. If he had done that with his gun drawn, we easily could have been in a shooting situation, and as much as I would have hated to shoot him, I certainly would have taken any actions necessary to ensure I would go home safely that night.

CHAPTER 41

Murder-for-Hire

Another unusual investigation that I was involved in was a murder-for-hire case in which there was a young man who was attempting to locate an assassin whom he could pay to kill his ex-girlfriend. The FBI learned about the plot from an informant, and we sent in an undercover agent who could participate in this plot and pretend to be a contract killer. We planned to build the case using acceptance of payments through the mail and using phone calls. In addition to attempted murder charges, prosecutors would then be able to pursue wire fraud charges. Accumulating evidence pertaining to this scheme was another example of how a case that ensures a criminal will go to jail is built. It is not just a simple matter of knowing about a wrongdoing and arresting somebody. Law enforcement has a terribly difficult burden of proof beyond a reasonable doubt, and by building cases with multiple charges, agents can increase the odds of having a successful prosecution. If a clever defense attorney figures out a technicality to evade one charge, then it is a luxury to have additional charges to fall back on that will help make sure justice is served.

This particular case called for many hours of surveillance. I was an able photographer and had previously shown my ability to take high quality photos with no setup or preparation time. I was relied upon to be able to get photos in high pressure surveillance situations, which could be later used as evidence in court. For this case we arranged a meeting on a Saturday afternoon between the subject and our undercover guy in a park in the town of Coronado near San Diego. The subject, who was in the military, was familiar with the park in Coronado since he had previously served nearby on this military-friendly island. I parked my car along the street where I could view our undercover agent as he met with the subject. I grabbed my Nikon D100 camera, clicked in a telephoto lens, and climbed into the back seat. I left a front window slightly cracked and positioned myself at an angle whereby I could zoom in on the meeting from the back seat with no distortion from window glass. However, despite the slighted opened front window, the interior of my vehicle's back seat quickly reached stifling triple-digit temperatures; although the outside summer air temperature was in the 80s, the sunbaked car interior was easily thirty degrees warmer. But there was little choice. I could not leave the car running or roll the windows down further or I would risk being spotted. Although I turned my FBI radio volume down so that it was barely audible inside my car, I still needed to communicate with the rest of the surveillance team and could not afford to have radio traffic drifting from wide open windows in the car.

I waited for the meet to occur. Despite the heat and my racing heart, I really enjoyed my position because it was exactly the work I had envisioned doing in the FBI. I was getting paid to take photos, so in a sense I was getting to be a professional photographer. These pictures would be used as evidence documenting criminal activity; this evidence would be used to take a potential killer off the street. The location on Coronado Island was a nice change from the usual seedy streets and rough areas where criminals typically hang out in the San Diego vicinity.

After about half an hour, the subject showed up with cash in hand. The fact hit me that he was actually attempting to pay somebody to murder another human being. I was thrilled to be part of the team that was putting a stop to this person's evil intent. I shot a number of photos; many were mediocre, but there were plenty that clearly showed the subject passing a cash payment to our undercover operative. After the meeting, we arrested the subject, and the case wound up being successfully prosecuted. I was proud to have contributed to this effort, and I knew that I had successfully taken surveillance photos that were one of the pieces of evidence that helped put this person behind bars.

CHAPTER 42

Things Change

One of the more popular sayings that I heard repeatedly in the FBI was: "If you aren't happy, just wait. And if you are happy, just wait." Things do change quickly in the FBI, from the cars agents are assigned to drive, to fellow squad members, to who the supervisor is. A change in supervisor can signal a significant change for everyone who reports to that supervisor. The FBI's operating structure follows a rigid model that is similar to that of a military organization. A supervisor position has great power and importance, since all activities that agents perform must be approved by a supervisor. All documents and papers must be reviewed by a supervisor. Short of going to the bathroom, anything an agent does has to be discussed with a supervisor.

I have always been self-motivated and worked well without close supervision. In fact, I have felt myself shut down creative thinking when closely watched, since I want to avoid criticism for "not doing it the supervisor's way." The FBI is very much a by-the-book organization, which combined with a strict supervisor can make an agent feel like a military member on a good day, and on a bad day feel like he or she is in a prison. I viewed micromanagement as a barrier, but I could see that close supervision keeps new agents from making mistakes and is an effective mechanism to keep a supervisor informed of the details for investigations that their agents perform.

During my time in San Diego I had four different supervisors, each with different management styles, but all fine agents in their own way. They had to manage a tricky balance between being too tough and too easygoing. My first two supervisors gave me free reign and allowed all of the agents on my squad to work on their own with as much autonomy as possible. These supervisors only tried to meet the minimum administrative requirements that all supervisors are responsible for, such as periodic case file reviews with the agents and authorization for specific types of investigative activities that are strictly governed by the FBI's rules. This approach resulted in the least amount of pressure and the most fun for agents. The feeling was not unlike having a substitute teacher when the usual teacher is out. After living through months of absolute military style regimentation at the FBI Academy, my day-to-day functions with my first two supervisors felt free and unrestricted. This made the job tolerable and encouraged me to work hard and follow the type of creativity that FBI agents are known for.

However, about six months into my stay in San Diego, my squad got a new supervisor, making this my third in six months (and counting my supervisor at the FBI Academy, this would be my fourth). This particular person was older and mature, but was used to operating on white collar squads that were much more regimented, with the complexity and details of long-term proactive investigations. He did not initially appreciate the dynamic nature of the reactive violent crime investigations that my squad performed. He demanded perfection, and was much more hands-on than my previous two supervisors. As a result, I felt that my work was administratively constrained; I no longer wanted to run out and chase bad guys or follow up on leads, since every action suddenly required another step in convincing our supervisor on actions we wanted to take. This same supervisor angered agents with his careful review and almost automatic rejection of the first draft of their written reports. He privately complimented my writing skills and always accepted my reports as-is; this made me happy to have his approval, but I did dread my encounters with him because it seemed that it was just a matter of time until he would anger me for being critical of a minor technical error.

But the FBI saying held true, and sure enough my squad received yet another supervisor a few months later; he would be my last supervisor in the Bureau before I decided to leave. My third supervisor had apparently became fed up with the constant barrage of activity that the violent crime squad endured on a 24/7 basis. While none of us had reason to question his hard work or good intent, none of my squad members were sad to see that supervisor move on to other opportunities more suited to his style. Looking back, I can appreciate his attention to detail, and his efforts to strive for excellence in the FBI.

My final supervisor, Supervisory Special Agent Allen Hobart, offered a reasonable balance of not being too particular with details but still wanting overall involvement or at least knowledge of our investigative activities. He was a former Marine, who immediately impressed me with his dedication, work ethic, and common sense. Aside from a tendency to use what many would deem as inappropriate language every few minutes, he was a dynamic leader and supervisor for the team. He had a true desire to be in his position, and did not treat it as just a stepping stone on his way to climb up the ranks in the FBI.

Allen had previously served as an agent working on drug investigations. He was more than familiar with how drug cartels operated, including the ancillary crimes that my squad was responsible for investigating, including kidnappings and Assault on Federal Officers (AFOs). He was well aware that the drug cartel members were heavily armed and frequently engaged in shootouts in Mexico. He knew that there was a significant risk of this violence spilling over to the United States side of the border, and he wanted to make sure agents on his squad were armed and prepared for any worst-case scenario.

Allen instructed all agents on the squad to acquire an extra weapon that would provide more firepower than our standard issue Glock handguns. I chose to carry an MP5, which I had received training on while attending the FBI Academy. The MP5 is a submachine gun that can shoot about 30 rounds in two seconds. This weapon is frequently shown in movies and television shows, in particular when depicting tactical operations such as SWAT teams. Although in the back of my mind I knew that I was getting this weapon for undesirable, dangerous reasons, I felt like a kid on Christmas morning when I picked up my gun from our tactical agent in charge of weapons. Having an MP5 was just plain cool. I could hardly wait to show Jennifer my new lethal toy. Upon seeing my weapon, she was unenthused because she knew that there was a reason that I was issued the gun; she did not want me have to use the MP5, or worse, have others use similar weapons on me.

This weapon became my new best friend in the FBI. Like a loyal pet, it would frequently ride with me in the passenger seat while I was performing operations. I kept it close since I knew that in an unexpected instant I might have to grab it and return fire from an attacker. The border violence was on the rise, and the operations I was part of were becoming increasingly frequent and hazardous. I carried this weapon for the remainder of my time in the FBI; if I did not have it in my passenger seat, I had it locked up in my trunk so that any time I was called out for an operation I would be armed and prepared. There were a number of occasions that I grabbed my MP5 and hunkered down in a car seat (sometimes front, sometimes back); I always hoped for the best but expected the worst. Thank goodness the worst never happened.

Allen also ensured that we received special tactical training that was similar to what I had undergone at the FBI Academy. Most agents graduating from the Academy are assigned to a squad, and rarely revisit the arrest tactics that they were trained on. The FBI focuses on firearms proficiency through mandatory quarterly tests, but an agent's tactical abilities are often untested until a real-life scenario unfolds. My squad did not need to have the extreme tactical training that the SWAT team requires, but we did find frequently find ourselves in dynamic arrest situations, and we needed to be able to work together as a tactical team when needed. Unlike my dislike of FBI Academy tactical training, I highly enjoyed taking a dedicated day in San Diego to train with my squad mates. These training sessions were far from relaxing and were packed with continuous observation and evaluation from SWAT tactical experts; however, any criticism offered was constructive rather than demeaning.

I wound up being assigned to use several different vehicles during my career in the FBI. Overall this is a fantastic benefit of being an FBI agent; the free car, gas, and insurance provided to agents helps to offset the relatively low pay that agents receive. My first vehicle, as previously mentioned, broke down during my first prisoner transport from Big Bear to San Diego. This incident proved that some of the older FBI vehicles were not reliable, and I certainly did not want to break down during a late-night trip out to the middle of the desert for an AFO investigation. If that happened, I would likely be out of cell phone and radio range, and my safety could be in serious jeopardy, especially if the drug cartels were operating nearby. There were areas of neighborhoods in San Diego, such as the Somali area we called "Little Mogadishu," that were scary merely to just drive through; the thought of breaking down and being on foot in that vicinity was unpleasant at best. A well-dressed, armed FBI agent is normally safe from criminals, but alone in the wrong area, he or she could easily be stuck in a bad situation. Part of being a good FBI agent is being finely tuned with what is called situational awareness. Agents who plan on successfully staying alive for their entire careers must be aware of their surroundings at all times and avoid dangerous situations through advanced planning and preparation. Driving an FBI vehicle that was on the verge of breaking down in a bad area went against everything that I had learned about improving my odds of staying safe. After discussion with my supervisor, I upgraded to a more reliable car.

And did I ever get a reliable workhorse. Yes, I was privileged to drive the mainstay of most police forces in the United States at the time, the one and only Ford Crown Victoria. It came fully equipped with the police package and was speedy for a large sedan. In my mind I kept replaying the lines from the movie *Blues Brothers* which references "cop tires, cop motor." And my Crown Vic even came with "cop lights" and a "cop siren!" A boyhood fantasy came true the first day that I slid behind the wheel and took it for a spin. I managed to find an empty parking lot, and I convinced myself that I should conduct training to practice flipping on the lights and siren. I even tried issuing commands over the built-in public address system (I am certain that shoppers in that plaza were puzzled to see a lone car with a guy shouting out "don't move, step out of the vehicle with your hands up," when there clearly were no other vehicles in the vicinity). I knew that in the future, when I pulled up to a bank robbery scene and stepped out with a suit on, there would be no question about who I was and why I was there. Although the unit was unmarked, the letters "FBI" might as well have been stamped on the side, and I was proud of it.

Because the vast majority of the population associates Crown Victoria cars with law enforcement, my beloved new car proved to be an extremely poor choice for surveillance operations. The windows were not tinted, the vehicle had an unusual police-style radio antenna sticking out, and there were "Police Interceptor" badges from the factory on the back. In the roughest San Diego neighborhoods this car would create interest from a mile away. Since working on arrest and surveillance operations was a significant part of how I spent my days, I quickly tired of having a vehicle that could prove to be a liability in many situations. On some squads this would serve as the perfect car, but for the violent crime squad, which often had overlap with undercover drug investigations, driving a Crown Vic was definitely not a practical method of transportation.

After a few months I was able to switch vehicles again. This time I was fortunate enough to receive an almost new Chrysler

Concorde, with nicely tinted windows and a CD player. I had been driving vehicles with excellent sound systems for fifteen years prior to joining the FBI, and despite the seemingly trivial nature of having fun music to listen to, I realized how much I missed simply being able to pop in a CD with my own tunes. This could really help pass the time for lengthy surveillance operations or merely for my daily commute to the office. Also, the car was not as obviously linked to law enforcement, and the tinted windows would make surveillance, including long-range photography, a much easier proposition. The car had previously been driven briefly by the Special Agent in Charge (SAC) of the office. He had passed the car along to the Assistant Special Agent in Charge (ASAC) over the criminal division in San Diego, and after the ASAC drove the car briefly, I was lucky enough to inherit it. This repeated pattern of "luck of the draw" was inherent in the FBI, ranging from cars to squad assignments to supervisors. While I would not consider myself lucky to be placed on a violent crime squad, I finally felt lucky in getting a nice, almost new car to drive.

One week later my good fortune changed and I wrecked the car. I was helping with surveillance on a bank robbery suspect and getting ready to assist with a dynamic rolling arrest. I was positioned towards the back of a line of unmarked FBI vehicles, all of which were waiting to move in quickly after the marked San Diego PD unit pulled over the subject. The arrest was about to occur on a busy four lane street. I was at a light and as I was turning left onto the four lane street, I floored the gas pedal and moved to the outside lane while passing a Buick that had just turned into the inside lane. Based on the snail's pace, I assumed that the driver of this Buick was an elderly person. He abruptly decided to take an immediate right turn from the outside lane, aiming directly for a Home Depot entrance, and he slammed into my car on the driver's side. But I was on a mission to arrive at the arrest scene and assist as needed. I did not know if I would be needed to stop traffic, or worst case, return fire to the subject, if things went awry. Knowing that the arrest was about to occur only a few blocks from that location, I made the immediate decision not to even lift my foot from the accelerator, and I sped away from the crash scene and headed to the arrest scene. I glanced in the rearview mirror and saw several cars come to a stop. Nobody appeared to be hurt from the impact, so I refocused on the arrest.

After arriving at the arrest scene, I saw that the subject had just been arrested without incident, and there were enough agents to direct traffic and search the subject's vehicle. I radioed my fellow agents and explained the situation regarding my accident, and I did a U-turn to head back to the accident scene. Although my adrenaline was flowing from both the accident and arrest, I tried to calm down so that I would not be unnecessarily rude to the person who had hit me. But in reality, I was furious. As an FBI agent, I was held to a higher standard than ordinary citizens or even other law enforcement officials; for the sake of all agents, I had to always maintain control and poise in any situation.

I rolled into the Home Depot parking lot and located the vehicle that hit me. An old man was the driver, and he had apparently reached an age where his mental and audible comprehension was lacking. He could barely understand that I was an FBI agent who had been about to assist with a bank robbery arrest. After explaining this several times, and after repeating myself multiple times concerning how he had tried to cross over a lane of traffic without signaling, he finally began to understand the damage he had done. Although he wound up paying for the damage to the car, there was no fix for my damaged pride. With an overwhelming feeling of dread, I keyed my microphone and had to report back to the San Diego office that I had just had an accident in my new car. To make matters worse, I remembered that I had my performance review coming up later in the week with my supervisor and, sure enough, the ASAC who had just handed down this vehicle to me. My good luck surely seemed short-lived.

Nevertheless, my review went well. I had established an

excellent reputation and had already completed and documented all of the requirements that the FBI wants new agents to be exposed to. In a span a few months I had already accumulated all of the variety of experiences that new agents are required to experience normally over a two year period. My squad saw approximately ten times more action than typical squads in the FBI. When I later met with the ASAC, he made complementary comments about my reputation and progress, and then changed to a serious tone and said, "Now, we do have the matter you wrecking my car." He shook his head for a few moments with a grave look on his face, and then burst into laughter. He knew that the accident was not my fault, and he reminded me that it was only a government vehicle that got some scars while fighting crime in the streets. He said I should be honored to have wrecked a car while arresting a bank robber. With a raised eyebrow, he concluded, "But don't do it again," as he wrapped up my otherwise glowing review.

CHAPTER 43

Traffic

The film *Traffic* is a favorite of mine. Long before I was in the FBI, I thoroughly enjoyed the performances of Benecio Del Toro, Michael Douglas, and Katherine Zeta-Jones in this film. The movie is an excellent depiction of the impact of drugs in the United States and the close linkage of the US drug trade to Mexico. I am used to Hollywood turning any realistic story into an exaggerated work of fiction that does not remotely resemble everyday life. However, after re-watching *Traffic* after working in the San Diego FBI office, I spotted filming locations such as the San Ysidro border crossing, where I know there are huge drug trafficking problems, and the gritty storyline closely paralleled real events that I had direct knowledge of. The high reward but high risk nature of the drug trade, along with the total destruction of families that have members that engage in using or trafficking drugs, is accurately reflected in the movie.

An incident that I was involved with that closely mirrored many of the events depicted in *Traffic* started as a kidnapping that was reported to the FBI. A high-ranking member of the largest drug cartel in the San Diego and Tijuana vicinity had been kidnapped, and there were huge monetary demands being made by the kidnappers. The subject had been missing several days, and his family had not wanted to report the kidnapping to the FBI for fear of the kidnappers finding out and killing their loved one. Moreover, they did not want to draw the attention of law enforcement on themselves. But in a moment of desperation and in recognition of the severity of their dilemma, the family knew they had little choice but to contact the FBI if they wanted to see their family member alive again.

The family initially contacted our office on a Friday afternoon, and we all realized that this could be a rare opportunity to nab kidnappers on US soil; while unlikely, there was at least the possibility that we could locate and rescue a victim. This immediately became the top priority case for the San Diego FBI.

We learned that the victim's family had agreed to pay out $200,000 to the kidnappers, and had agreed to provide those funds on a Saturday, which was the after the kidnapping was reported to the FBI. By the following morning, the family had already accumulated the ransom money in cash at a business that they owned, and several agents, including me, went to assist with picking up the money. We were on high alert and were ready to return fire if violence erupted. Any time hundreds of thousands of dollars of cash are involved, there is potential for violence. After picking up the money and returning to the FBI building, we counted the cash. The bills were all $20 denomination, which took about an hour to count using three agents. The cash drop deadline was looming, and we did not have time to record the serial number from each bill, so in a pinch I decided to take some photos of the cash. Although I did not know if this would be important or useful later on, I figured the photos would at least reveal the serial numbers of bills that were placed at the top of each bundle.

The cash was placed in a special bag that had a transmitter sewn into the lining. The bag looked like an ordinary gym bag, but the signal would be tracked by the FBI with the hope of finding the kidnappers and possibly the victim. My entire squad, along with the FBI SWAT team and other available agents, was activated to help with the operation.

While surveillance agents departed to watch the ransom drop-off, which would be done by a male relative of the victim, another agent and I stayed behind with the wife of the victim near the FBI office. Her demeanor was quite calm considering the situation. Her clothing and accessories provided clues indicating that this woman was wealthy. Her approach was business-like and it did not convince me that she was dedicated to her husband in the traditional sense; the attitude and mannerisms that she conveyed demonstrated a level of concern that I would expect to see while someone awaits receiving the bill when bringing in a car for a transmission repair. She kept her phone close by in case the kidnappers tried to contact her. She asked me what the chances of successfully recovering her husband alive were. I told her that in all honesty, based on my experience, successful recovery of a victim is rare. I tried to prepare her for the worst, but she appeared to have already come to terms with her husband's predicament.

I listened to the real-time radio chatter of the FBI surveillance team. To our dismay, the team lost sight of the ransom payment. The kidnappers had called the relative who was dropping off the cash, carefully instructed him to park behind a big-box store next to a sheet metal fence, and then had him walk from his vehicle through a narrow opening in the fence to deliver the cash. Our agents not only did not have visibility behind the store, but they had absolutely no way of observing what was happening behind the fence. The subjects grabbed the cash and left the relative empty-handed. As they fled, the signal from the transmitter in the bag grew faint and quickly died, leaving the FBI and therefore me in a horrible position of telling the victim's spouse that we lost the signal, lost the cash, and lost our best chance to rescue her husband. This definitely ranked as one of my lowest moments of being an FBI agent.

All available agents were instructed to head to the drop-off area as quickly as possible and to fan out while listening to our radios for the transponder signal. There would be a "beep" that could be heard on one of our encrypted radio channels, and as the transmitter got closer the frequency of beeps would increase. At this point there were probably twenty vehicles being driven by FBI agents who were desperately circling around the area. I knew that agents were crossing paths and had saturated a several square mile area, so I decided to take a different approach and head to roads that are directly on the border. If the kidnappers were attempting to flee the United States, I figured I might be able to pick up a signal before they could leave the country, in time to intercept them. I drove around a couple of hours on back roads that were unfamiliar. I wound up at the Border Field State Park, on the coast of California, on the border directly between San Diego and Tijuana. It was a beautiful but ominous location. There was a wall of giant metal beams erected in the sand to divide the United States and Mexico. Seeing the columns that looked like gigantic vertical jail bars was a striking and sad sight. It made me hope that one day the violence and poverty in Mexico will die down to a level at which the United States can truly embrace our neighbors to the south without fear of damaging our own country.

Although I had no luck picking up the signal, I finally heard the news come over my radio that the signal had almost miraculously been located, and that the surveillance team had determined which vehicle the signal was coming from. The surveillance team followed this vehicle and driver to various locations, including shopping malls. All of the agents stayed in the nearby vicinity of the subject's vehicle; little did the public know that scores of FBI agents were flooding the roads in Chula Vista on that sunny afternoon.

Finally, FBI agents followed the subject's vehicle to a residence. The subject parked the vehicle and disappeared into the house, which we hoped would contain additional kidnappers and the kidnap victim. Since there had been other kidnap victims reported under very similar circumstances, we all knew that this house could hold the key to solving a number of other unsolved kidnapping investigations. Other subjects were spotted entering and leaving the house; the FBI did not know the identities of these people, but we had to assume that they were part of the kidnapping conspiracy. We would have loved to continue surveillance for several days, which would have allowed us to identify as many parties involved with the kidnapping as possible. We could have tracked their movements, locations, and potentially, even their associations with other criminals. However, we knew that time was of the essence for the victim, assuming he was still alive, and that since the ransom had been paid, we needed to act immediately in case the kidnappers planned to kill him.

As vehicles left the house, the FBI SWAT team members, who had split into several smaller groups, pulled over and arrested the drivers when they were out of visual and audible range from the house. I assisted with one of these arrests, which was fun to watch. A couple of hulking dark Chevy Suburbans blocked the street and FBI SWAT members in full tactical gear ran up to the vehicle with assault rifles pointed at the driver. They were yelling commands and all were ready to engage in battle if needed. The driver wisely followed commands, turned off the engine, put his hands in the air, and completely surrendered to the arresting agents. This arrest occurred at an intersection in a busy street, so I popped my strobe lights on, jumped out of the car, and started directing traffic around the scene. I tried to keep a straight face but my excitement overwhelmed me, and I could not help myself from mentally replaying the Leslie Nielsen line from *Naked Gun,* "Nothing to see here, move along, move along," as he ushers along onlookers who are gawking at fireworks plant exploding in the background. This was not quite a fireworks show, but it was probably more law enforcement action that these drivers had ever seen. FBI SWAT made several other arrests, which made for an unusually productive day for that group. Like a pack of dogs that have been trained and are finally released for a hunt, the SWAT team members clearly were enjoying their line of work on that occasion.

The FBI generally discourages agents from dynamically entering (or "storming") houses. The risk to agents, victims, and subjects dramatically increases when agents must venture into an unknown structure. However, for the safety of the victim, the decision was made to proceed with dynamically entering the house. I listened breathlessly on my radio as I heard the tactical "execute" command, signaling agents to move in. As the team hit the house from the front, a subject emerged from the back of the house and took off on foot. An FBI sniper was watching this activity through his scope from several hundred yards away. Rather than allowing the subject to escape, the agent sprinted to the house, took off in the direction that the subject had gone, and ran him down. While this tactic is not encouraged by the FBI, nobody was second guessing the decision when he marched the subject in handcuffs back to the scene. With a wide grin, his pride in safely apprehending the subject was apparent. For me, this was just another example of how FBI agents risk their lives to protect others. FBI SWAT team members are no joke.

Upon entering the house, the SWAT team located a young man wearing handcuffs; he claimed to be a kidnap victim. After further searching the house, the team found another person in handcuffs in a closet; he appeared to be in worse physical condition than the original victim they had encountered. After interviewing both people, agents determined that the first one found was actually the primary kidnapper, who was only pretending to be a victim in a desperate attempt to save his own skin. This cowardly act and blatant lie did not surprise anyone; agents are trained always to question what they are told. I put my set of handcuffs on the kidnapping subject, and removed the other set of handcuffs that belonged to the kidnapper, to be held as evidence. A search revealed cash in his pocket, and a later comparison of serial numbers revealed a match to one of the photos I had taken of the ransom money. There was no doubt that this was the kidnapper.

As the sun went down and evening began, I saw exhaustion on the faces of the agents at the scene. I knew that all of us had a long night ahead of us for gathering evidence, conducting interviews, and handling the arrested subjects. For several hours I was responsible for the custody of the kidnapper. While radioing back to personnel in the office, I learned that he was believed to be responsible for numerous other kidnappings and killings, including gruesome murders which had resulted in discovery of bodies with severed heads found in trunks. These were killings that we were aware of in the United States; we had no idea how many other victims had died at his hands in Mexico. I was disgusted with this person, but I attempted some conversation with him, hoping he would open up and admit to his crimes. He pretended that he had no idea what was going on; he claimed to be completely puzzled about why he had been arrested. I merely responded with, "Ok, good luck with that line of defense." He later asked if I could remove his handcuffs, which I had used to restrain him with his hands behind his back per FBI policy, and allow him to be re-cuffed with his hands in front so he would be more comfortable. I did not even respond to his question. I was tempted to tighten up the cuffs and ask him how it felt, but I maintained my professionalism. But the fact that many deaths were on his hands and that he had just held and tortured a kidnapped man for over a week never strayed from my mind. I looked forward to seeing the wheels of justice crush this sick, evil individual.

The subjects and victim were all finally taken to the San Diego Police Department headquarters. I got to spend many hours with the victim at SDPD, and despite his history of criminal involvement, he seemed like a relatively ordinary guy. We found that we shared a common love of off-road motor sports; he was a former Baja trophy truck driver and had previously raced motocross. As I had seen before, being able to establish a normal conversation with this person paid off. After a couple of hours he opened up to me that he had been involved with some illegal dealings that were what ultimately put him in this position, and he vowed to come clean and help the FBI to understand more about how the criminal organizations, or drug cartels, that he was aware of operate. He was truly grateful for his life being saved and at that moment I believe that he was sincere in his comments, although I did not expect him to incriminate himself or further elaborate on illegal activities that he was directly involved in.

Part of the evening's duties were to photograph and document the injuries that the victim had sustained while being held. He not only had painful marks where handcuffs had restrained him, but also he had a number of bruises and scratch marks from being repeatedly hit with an electric stun-gun. There was no question that he had effectively been tortured by the kidnappers. This further showed me how lucky he was just to be alive, let alone able to walk and with all of his limbs and fingers intact. But I also knew that even if the damage to his skin healed in a few weeks, the mental toll of being captured and tortured could stay with him for life.

In the meantime, the victim's wife was notified that her husband was alive and safe, but that he was still being held at SDPD to be questioned about the kidnapping events. The victim and his wife owned a restaurant in Mexico, and that night someone fired into the building with a machine gun. I would later learn that two people had been killed at the restaurant, and somebody left barrels of acid that had been used to get rid of dead bodies. The victim wound up having to shut down his restaurant. My brain conjured images of another horrible scene that would have fit right into the movie *Traffic*. The risk of violence and retaliation against the victim for working with the FBI was so dangerous that the San Diego Police Department stationed officers with machine guns around the San Diego Police Department building. There was a great possibility of retaliation from the drug cartel members against the victim and his associates, and United States law enforcement was now in a position to be caught right in the middle of that violence. Around that time, I would typically see an article about once per week with a horrible story about Mexican law enforcement officials being shot and killed in gun battles. Suddenly, the likelihood of a similar scenario playing out on our side of the border seemed to be a real possibility.

Finally, as of that Sunday morning around 7:00 a.m., we

were finally finished with interviewing the victim, and we were ready to head to a hotel at an undisclosed location for the victim to be reunited with his wife. My partner and I drove out of the SDPD building garage with the victim in the back seat. We had our eyes open and were ready to draw our guns in an instant if we were attacked, but luckily we never had to remove our guns from our holsters. But every car that drove by us caused me to have concern, and I kept imagining armed men rolling down their windows and opening fire on us. We arrived safely at the hotel, and walked with the victim into the lobby. After saying our goodbyes and hearing a final round of sincere thanks from the victim and his family, we departed and finally were heading back to our homes to get some much needed sleep.

Over the next couple of days, starting with later that Sunday afternoon, we worked with other agents to piece together what had happened and to write our reports. We found out that the victim had been lured to a house by a young and attractive woman, but instead of finding her there alone, he found himself in a nest of kidnappers. The kidnapping group had used the same method to capture dozens of others, and most of those victims had ultimately been tortured and killed. In another life-imitating-art style twist, the primary kidnapper, whom I had to babysit after his arrest turned out to be gay, just like the assassin in the movie *Traffic*. He was thin, healthy, and at times even personable. Yet he was a cold-blooded killer operating on United States soil. As previously mentioned, the Mexican drug war has claimed tens of thousands of lives. If the United States does not invest significant resources to combat similar drug related violence here in our country, I fear that we will eventually suffer a fate similar to Mexico's.

CHAPTER 44

White Collar, Cyber, and Violent Crime

While I tended to violent criminal matters on a daily basis, I did my best to supplement my FBI experience with white-collar and cyber-crime, exposure which I thoroughly enjoyed. One of the white-collar crime cases that I was exposed to began in the form of a phone call to me at 4:00 a.m. on an early Saturday morning. I had just began a weekly cycle of being the designated after-hours duty agent, which meant that for a week I would receive all after-hours calls to the FBI in San Diego. The call began as a reported kidnapping, which was my area of expertise. However, the core elements of the crime wound up being linked to a group of criminals who were performing mortgage fraud. A disagreement over unpaid money between criminal partners had resulted in a kidnapping; the victim (who was also involved with fraudulent mortgage schemes) was taken to Mexico, but he had escaped. However, attempting to enter the United States, he had been caught by the Customs and Border Patrol agents, at which point the FBI was called in. Although it was not even 5:00 a.m., I began to get dressed and headed towards the border to start piecing together the details.

After a whirlwind of interviews and arrests related to the kidnapping, I was able to piece together an elaborate criminal conspiracy that involved getting straw buyers to purchase flipped houses at prices that were greatly over the actual home value. These phony buyers would take out fraudulent loans for the entire inflated home value amount and purchase the home from crooked sellers. The sellers would then have a gigantic amount of cash from the sale that they would split with the buyers. These homes would then be abandoned, and the straw buyers would just take a hit on their credit; this downside did not outweigh the tens of thousands of dollars they would gain on one fraudulent real estate transaction. The crooked sellers would not have appeared to have broken any laws, which provided a relatively low-risk and high-reward scheme. It was obvious that these criminals had performed this scam multiple times, easily resulting in hundreds of thousands of dollars of fraud. On a national level, this type of fraud was likely in the billions annually, and played a part in the financial crisis that plagued the United States around that time. However, after talking with a white collar crime supervisor in the FBI, I learned that if I did not have direct evidence that clearly showed a crime of seven figures, the FBI did not have the resources to investigate. This was infuriating, although I understood the limited resources constraint all too well. A criminal could rob a bank and nab $800 in cash and have dozens of agents and police hunting him down, but $800,000 in mortgage fraud did not even merit the opening of a formal investigation. This was frustrating and eye-opening, and helped me to see that the grass would not be much greener (or more satisfying) working white collar or cybercrime.

The subjects, including an older "wise guy" from the East Coast who seemed straight out of *The Sopranos*, spent eight months in jail awaiting trial. Since I was the case agent and had been present during most of the events that made the case, I wound up testifying at length in preliminary hearings, which were held prior to the actual trial. The preliminary hearing allowed attorneys to learn more about the opposing side's case and often would help both sides reach a plea agreement and avoid the expense and uncertainty of a full trial.

I found testifying to be one of the most taxing duties that I had during my time in the FBI. For this case, I had to testify for approximately two hours straight, covering elements of the crime, which spanned multiple locations, multiple subjects, and multiple storylines, in laborious detail. Trying to keep all of the facts straight while being scrutinized by the defense attorneys was unpleasant and demanding. Naturally, they attempted to rattle me and challenged me every step of the way. Adding to the complexity, since the case had gone to the State of California for prosecution, as opposed the Federal court system, there were different rules for testifying that I had to be aware of and take into consideration. This made for exhausting days and sleepless nights. My testimony wound up being sufficient for the case to proceed with a full trial.

But after spending a number of weeks working with the San Diego District Attorney's Office preparing for the case, right before the trial, a key witness refused to testify. Although he had been subpoenaed, the subpoena was issued by the State of California and did not technically hold any legal ground in Missouri, where this criminal had relocated. I strongly suspected that he was still in communication with the subjects who would soon be on trial, and surmised that possibly he had been provided financial incentives not to cooperate. Other witnesses suddenly could not be located. It was as if all parties with any knowledge of the crimes fell off the face of the earth, except for the criminals who were in prison. Unfortunately, we knew that the witness testimony would be critical in obtaining a guilty verdict, so after unsuccessfully sending out leads to other FBI field offices to locate witnesses, the DA decided to drop the case. So from the standpoint of the criminals, the entire enterprise could pick back up with their mortgage fraud scheme relatively unscathed. I was outraged, because I could see that even with an exhaustive knowledge of their crimes, the government was not in a position to stop them. I felt particularly bad for the bright, energetic lawyers from the DA's office who had spent countless hours on the case, only to have it dismissed. As I would learn on numerous occasions, the cards in the legal system are greatly stacked in favor of the accused. The system is far from perfect; there are rare incidents of innocent people being convicted of a crime that they did not commit, which is a horrible crime in itself. But on the flip side, I know that for every criminal behind bars, there are probably hundreds still on the streets committing crimes.

Part IV

The End of the FBI Dream

CHAPTER 45

Calling it Quits

After all of the excitement of numerous all-night (and sometimes all-weekend) sessions of chasing the bad guys, I was ready to call it quits. I had been living the FBI life for almost two years, and despite the excitement and occasional job satisfaction, chasing violent criminals for the next twenty years did not sound appealing. While I still enjoyed getting to carry my credentials and was proud to announce to people that I was an FBI agent, I felt that in the grand scheme, I was not making much of a difference in the world. After the course of almost two years in the FBI, I knew that the job was not something that I woke up in the morning and looked forward to. I did not see how I could truly embrace a job with unsolved kidnappings and violent crimes; I did not know how to just "shelve" the emotions on a weekend or evening and pick back up the following day. Many people in the FBI really do not have any personal life or family to speak of, and for those individuals the FBI may be fantastic profession. Other agents with families make difficult sacrifices and put their country first, and are mentally tough enough to compartmentalize what happens on the job, or else simply have the fortitude to keep going despite mental exhaustion or disillusion.

Was my desire to fight for truth, justice, and the American way not on par with that of other FBI agents who refused to quit and continue to serve in this difficult profession? I had to ask myself this question, and I can look at myself in the mirror knowing the honest answer. My desire was not the problem. I had watched every episode of the Discovery Channel's *FBI Files* documentary show at least once. When I had arrived at the FBI Academy, one of my FBI agent counselors had been heavily involved with one of the cases depicted on *FBI Files*. I could scarcely believe that I was getting into a profession that I had dreamed about for years. This counselor told me that what when I graduated from the FBI Academy, life would be fulfilling and that he looked forward to every single day as an FBI agent. I believed him, which only set my expectations much higher than they should have been. Unfortunately, his circumstances were quite different from mine. He was assigned to a rural area in the Midwest, and his job largely consisted of driving around to making "house calls" to small-town and rural police insurance departments. While being in a position to help coordinate law enforcement in rural areas was important, this was a far cry from the stress of being placed on a violent crime squad on the border of Mexico.

Since it had been so incredibly difficult to get into the FBI, I exhausted every route that I could to find happiness within the Bureau. I attempted to switch to a white-collar squad, which would have complex and challenging investigations, but would have provided an improved work / life balance. I located a new agent who had recently been assigned to a white-collar squad and was unhappy with her assignment. She was single and wanted more action as an agent, so we both agreed that we would swap positions if the FBI management would allow us to do so. Both of our supervisors were initially on board, and my hopes were high that I would be able to start a new chapter in my career as an FBI agent. However, management at a level above our supervisors put a stop to our request. The reasoning was that there were other factors to be considered, such as other agents who were more senior than we were, who deserved the first shot at changing squads. I wholeheartedly agreed with that assessment from a logical perspective; I did not deserve any preferential treatment and did feel that the men and women who had put in years of dedication with the FBI should have the first choice on squad assignments. However, I was disappointed not to see any changes in squad personnel over the next few months; I had taken the initiative to make a positive change for another agent and myself, and yet my request was denied by an administrator who apparently had looked at the request as a "what if" scenario, and had chosen to protect himself from looking bad if somebody had complained about my transfer. When I saw no movement for agents to be reassigned to squads based on their preferences, that enforced my negative view of the vast FBI administrative bureaucracy, and made me feel that if I could not make a difference in my own life in the FBI, how could I really make an impact on the outside world?

Another factor that was preventing my transfer from the squad was the simple fact that the violent crime squad was vastly understaffed. There was far more work to be done than the available resources could accomplish. We could only afford the time to react to major violent crimes, but there were a number of proactive investigations that we did not have the manpower to work. To make matters worse, kidnappings and drug-related violence were on the rise, without an end in sight. My squad could not afford to lose agents, or more importantly, the knowledge and experience that agents rapidly gained in working violent crimes. Violent crimes tend to grab headlines, and I did not blame the FBI management for wanting to make sure that we were covered for high-media exposure events. While I saw the immediate need to add more agents on my squad, I also recognized a tremendous need for more agents in other areas, especially for white collar crimes, including cyber-crime, mortgage fraud, corporate fraud, and health-care fraud. The FBI had reacted to some extent to these growing criminal trends, but it seemed to me that the Bureau was only scratching the surface of all the crimes that were being committed. Based on my computer and corporate background, I knew that I would have been able to make a more significant contribution by working unaddressed white collar crimes instead of violent crimes. Seeing my best skills go to waste with reactive investigations that could have often been handled by local law enforcement officials did not encourage me to continue my role in the FBI.

I had a number of broad improvement ideas that I knew would never be realized; it is difficult for a low-level FBI agent to make or even suggest changes that impact the organization. For example, in the cyber-crime realm, I felt that the squad should be split up with specialized agents assigned to different squads using a classic matrix organization structure that is common in the corporate world. A "computer crime" was logically the same as a "telephone crime" or "mail crime", and the FBI certainly did not have dedicated squads for telephone or mail crimes. There was a need for more technological expertise throughout all squads. However, unlike in my previous jobs, in which I could make a positive suggestion that would be entertained seriously by the highest levels of the organization, the FBI management was resistant to change and effectively sent the message to agents: "You do your job, and let us do ours." From day one, I always understood and accepted that my assignments would be based on "the needs of the Bureau." But I also understood that despite the similarities, the FBI is not the military; I was free to leave at any time. The more time I spent in danger and away from my family, the more I was convinced that leaving the Bureau was the right move for me.

My long-term plan in the FBI was eventually to transfer to the Austin FBI office, which is a satellite office of the San Antonio Division. Unfortunately, the wait for agents to transfer to Austin was projected at twenty years; this office had the highest demand in the Bureau. In twenty years I planned on being retired. I knew that I could get to one of the Texas border cities much faster, which could potentially result in with an Austin transfer before I hit twenty years, but that plan was filled with uncertainly. I knew that an assignment to any border city would likely be a miserable experience of working the same types of illegal border activity that I wanted to get away from in San Diego. I did not see myself wanting to stay in San Diego serving on the violent crime squad for an extended length of time. I was effectively out of viable options in the FBI, and I realized that it was time to begin exploring outside employment. For the first time since applying to the FBI, I dusted off my resume and updated it with my FBI employment experience.

Although I began to look outside of the FBI for a new job, an opening in the Austin office came open for an analyst, and while the jump from agent to analyst almost never occurs, I felt that for me this would be a great fit. I was emotionally mature enough not to care that the general "pecking order" in the FBI places the status of agents above analysts and other employees. And I knew that a good analyst could actually make a greater impact than an entire squad of agents who only respond to individual crimes without seeing a bigger picture that could lead to dismantling an entire criminal enterprise. I spoke with the lead agent in Austin, who encouraged me to apply for the job. I followed the standard application process, which was the same process that any citizen undergoes when applying for an FBI job, and never heard back. I took this as a sign that I should move on to other things.

Jennifer continually worried about my safety and was frequently disappointed on weekends when my job interfered with our plans. Aside from my personal unhappiness, I knew that it was not fair to her to continue in my profession. We were tired of living with our four animals, two Chinese Pug dogs and two Persian cats, in small quarters that we could barely afford. We were tired of having a window-unit air conditioner that struggled to cool our living room. We had been used to living in a spacious house before moving to California. A brief time in an apartment was fine, but over time we grew to miss our creature comforts and the privacy and security that a comfortable house offers. I even felt bad for our animals, who went from having a house with windows and views to a small apartment with nothing to look at but off-white walls. We missed Texas; friends, family, food, open spaces, and friendly people were all elements that seemed to be absent in California.

In the meantime, Jennifer had a network of former coworkers who were more than eager to have her return to working at Dell. We had kept our house in Austin and rented it out, knowing that if we were unhappy with the FBI, we could have a place to land in Texas. Within a few weeks of looking, she found a job at Dell, with part of the deal a package that would cover our move back to Texas. We had a home to live in, a job, and expenses paid for; there was nothing else to do but for me to make that final decision on whether I really was going to leave the FBI, which would be the end of a lifetime dream.

CHAPTER 46

Resignation

Despite a list of "cons" that greatly outnumbered the "pros," I still had to do long hours of agonizing soul-searching to make the firm decision to leave. I asked my other agents about how they felt about their jobs. I received a number of private comments from agents that they were unhappy, that they missed their old professions, and that they now felt locked into being FBI agents since the pay ramps up quickly in the first five years and they are dependent on the relatively high salary, typically well over $100,000 per year, that more seasoned agents make. Their thoughts and support helped me reach the conclusion that I was not completely crazy for wanting to leave a job that I thought would be my ultimate dream come true. At the FBI Academy, the instructors continually reminded us that the FBI interview process is really for the first two years, which is a probationary period. The FBI has the right to terminate employment of any agents that are not performing adequately during that time period (firing becomes more difficult beyond the two-year probationary period). I had nearly flawless reviews and was well liked and respected by my superiors in San Diego. I had completed all of the new agent requirements. I had an excellent performance record and passed the FBI's long-term interview with flying colors. But in my mind the interview worked both ways. And in some areas the FBI had received unacceptably low marks from my perspective.

We decided to pull the trigger on our plan to get back to Texas. Jennifer formally accepted a job back in Austin. The time had arrived for me to give notice of my resignation. I stayed awake almost the entire night prior to informing my supervisor. Making things worse, my supervisor had gone for three weeks on vacation. I had wanted to talk to him face-to-face, but with the timing of Jennifer's job, we could not afford to wait three weeks to do so. After envisioning an incredibly painful resignation conversation dozens of times throughout the night, the morning light finally came, and it was time to make the call. First I drove to the office and sat in my car. My hand was trembling and heart was racing. I felt sick at my stomach and sat staring at my cell phone for over an hour. Things would never be the same after this call. I would never achieve a lifetime dream again like joining the FBI. Once I left, that dream would be cold and dead. I could not help but keep mentally calling myself a quitter. I had to concentrate on the list of "cons" about the FBI, and think through my decision from a logical standpoint; if I had only relied on an emotional decision, I would not have been able to place that call. I felt like a rock star calling his agent saying, "I changed my mind, I'm not performing." Or an astronaut calling NASA and saying, "On second thought, I don't think going into space is for me." Or the politician elected to a high office after a brutal campaign saying, "You know, I really don't want to be a senator after all." Despite feeling like a lunatic who might be making a huge mistake, I finally entered my supervisor's telephone number, and clicked on the green "call" button to call it quits.

My supervisor's wife answered the call with a friendly "hello." She informed me that her husband was out playing tennis, but she would take a message, and he would call me back. The pain I felt while waiting for the call back made me wish I was doing anything else; I would have preferred going through another defensive tactics class complete with bloody knuckle pushups and screaming instructors rather than face my supervisor with the news that I was leaving. Two nerve-wracking hours later, my supervisor called back and I was finally able to tell him that I was resigning. My supervisor was very gracious and understanding, and said that knowing me, he was certain that I had already thought through my decision carefully and that it was a personal decision. After hanging up the phone, I felt flooded with relief. No regrets. No remorse. A weight had been lifted. I felt overwhelming happiness and a sense of freedom that I had not felt since joining the FBI.

Next, I informed my relief supervisor that I was resigning, and told him that I had already spoken with our normal supervisor. I had additional conversations with the some of the senior management in San Diego. Some gave me "tough sell" speeches and tried to get me to stay. They knew I had a flawless record and reputation. But my mind was made up, and they ultimately accepted my decision.

One afternoon, the new SAC, Kevin Slatter, came down to my office area and wished me a happy birthday (which happened to occur just after I resigned), and told me that he heard that I was leaving. He was incredibly understanding and gracious; he wanted to know informally if there was anything that could have been done to keep me as an agent. I told him that the root cause of my unhappiness was my assignment to a violent crime squad, which I could not get away from. The FBI made assignments to squads strictly based on the current needs of the Bureau, but without regard for an agent's background. If I had received an assignment that was more in line with my white collar and computing skills, I would have been able to make a more significant contribution to the Bureau, and I likely would have been happier. SAC Slatter and other senior managers seemed to really listen to my input. A few months after I left, I learned that the FBI changed their new agent assignment process so that new agents would be informed of their first type of assignment before setting foot in the FBI Academy. While this change may have been coincidence, I would like to think that in at least a small way I played a role in the FBI that would lead to more effective assignments for future agents, leading to happier careers and a better FBI.

CHAPTER 47

Last Hurrah

Although I had provided two weeks' notice that I was leaving the Bureau, I continued to be heavily utilized for FBI operations after I turned in my resignation. My last arrest occurred less than one week before my last day as an agent. For several months I had been working a complex case that involved a kidnapping plot that was devised by a former Secret Service agent. He was working with a man from Kentucky, the former boyfriend of a woman in San Diego. The overall plan they devised was to kidnap the woman while she was on vacation in Mexico using phony Mexican police. The fake Mexican cops would hold her on a trumped-up drug charge, and they would demand to have hundreds of thousands of dollars wired to them by the woman's wealthy parents.

My partner Mark and I had arrested the former Secret Service agent, and we had traveled to Kentucky to locate the other man and interview him. We wound up speaking with this man for many hours over the course of two days. We even arranged to have a polygraph test conducted for him. He had the ability to easily create explanations that concealed his true actions; if channeled correctly, he would have been considered by most to be an incredibly gifted, talented, and imaginative storyteller. If this man could have put his ideas down on paper as fiction, he could have become the next Stephen King or Tom Clancy. Unfortunately, we did not have sufficient backing from the prosecutor from the United States Attorney's Office arrest him immediately, but we continued to monitor his location after we concluded our trip to Kentucky. Sure enough, he unwisely ventured to the San Diego vicinity, and we became concerned for the safety of the woman who had been the target of the original kidnapping plan. After a thorough review of the evidence in the case, including new information that we gained while in Kentucky, the United States Attorney's Office backed our decision to arrest the man and charge him as part of a kidnapping conspiracy.

I was less than excited to be participating in this final arrest. I was somewhat superstitious about my safety; I had navigated nearly two years of guns, arrests, and danger, and squeezing in "just one more" arrest seemed to be tempting fate. Jennifer showed even less enthusiasm for this development. She wanted me to refuse to participate since I was leaving anyway. But I wanted to end my short career on a positive note, and this arrest would help provide closure not only for this particular case, but for me personally.

We devised a creative plan to arrest this individual safely by employing the help of our friends at the California Highway Patrol, known as "Chippies." We used a ruse of having the "Chippies" call Lane to tell him that he needed to swing by a CHP substation to fix a problem with his driver's license and receive a new license. My partner and I waited in the office of a CHP supervisor for the subject to arrive. Once he did, he was directed into the office, and his face immediately fell when he saw us. He gave a valiant and ingenious effort to talk his way out of being arrested, but there was no way we were leaving the building without having him in handcuffs.

I got behind the wheel of my partner's brand new Chrysler 300 and tried my best to soak in the experience while I drove the subject to the federal prison. I led my last prisoner into the prison in what I hoped would be my last visit to any penitentiary for the rest of my life. The sun had disappeared behind the vast expanse of the Pacific Ocean. Although I had a few more administrative days as an agent, I felt my career come to a close as the evening yielded to darkness.

CHAPTER 48

Adios, California; Hello, Texas

My last day as an FBI agent finally arrived, and I had to turn in my badge, credentials, and gun. This was surprisingly not as emotionally draining as I had imagined; I simply handed over these items to my ASAC and signed some paperwork, and I was done. I also turned in a pair of handcuffs, although thanks to my excellent partner agent Janet, who provided a spare set of cuffs to me for this purpose, I was able to keep my personal handcuffs that I had been using from the FBI Academy all the way to my last arrest. These cuffs remain a cherished souvenir of my time in the FBI.

I never lost my sense of humor during my time in the FBI. I decided to leave one last going-away prank for my coworkers. Several days before my final day, I had figured out how to write an email and schedule delivery for a future date using Microsoft Outlook. My inner humor writer kicked in, and I composed an outrageous fictitious story about why I was leaving. My message was delivered a week later when I was back in Texas, and the feedback I received was that most recipients had a tremendous laugh when they read it, but some of the management was not at all pleased that a former employee was somehow able to send out an email on a strictly internal FBI system which I no longer had access to. I was glad to solidify my reputation as being a person with humor and cleverness, one who marches to the beat of his own drum.

As a testament to the good nature of my fellow coworkers and agents, there was a large going-away celebration held for me on my last day. Although I felt like I was abandoning these dedicated people who would continue to fight crime, they still were willing to celebrate my departure. There are no words that can express my appreciation for this. Not only did it make me feel well liked, but it helped me to hold my head high as I departed my life of fighting crime for a new chapter in my life. After a number of handshakes, hugs, and even a few tears, I said goodbye to this incredible group of people who had been my friends and family in California. Although I would never see most of them again, I would also never forget them, nor would I forget the sacrifices that they personally continue to make for the sake of this country. These FBI employees that make a choice every day to sacrifice themselves, be it physically or emotionally, for the benefit of others are true heroes.

Jennifer and I had been packing and preparing for our move back to Texas. We loaded up our animals early on a Saturday morning, the day after my last day in the FBI, and departed San Diego. The view of San Diego in the mirror was a relief but also haunting at the same time. We had driven in on the same highway less than two years earlier, with joy and high hopes for a rewarding life in California. This was truly the end of an era. However, even if this door was closing, another door had opened for us back in Texas, and I was ready to step through that door and begin a new life.

It took less than twenty four hours of leaving the FBI to be reminded that I was no longer part of the law enforcement community. Driving back to Texas, I was pulled over in a stretch of highway in New Mexico for speeding. The speed limit on Interstate 10 was eighty miles per hour, which was a safe speed to travel for the vast and unpopulated stretches that are found throughout the southwestern United States. Thinking that I was obeying the law, I missed seeing a sixty five miles per hour sign in a tiny desert town that consisted of a gas station and a bar. I saw flashing lights, pulled over, and was informed that I was speeding. I had to laugh to myself because as an agent I had sped on countless occasions and never once been pulled over.

The cop was cordial, but I had the primal feeling return to me that "cops are the enemy" as he scrawled out a ticket. I was no longer an FBI agent, part of a brotherhood of people who risk their lives to fight crime. I had rejoined the ranks of the average citizens who flash lights to each other when approaching a speed trap, and generally have an "us versus them" attitude towards the police, despite the difficult job and sacrifices that are made by law enforcement every day for the safety and benefit of the public.

We finally crossed the Texas state line, and Jennifer and I felt a sense of excitement and relief. We stopped at a Texas Roadhouse restaurant, and the food and service could not have been better. We were in high spirits, and elated to be back in the state we considered our home. I cannot adequately describe the sense of relief knowing that I truly would no longer have to answer middle-of-the-night emergency phone calls. There would be no more interruptions of our weekend or vacation plans. I would not be thrust into a spur-of-the-moment situation where it was up to me to use my gun to try to stop a deadly encounter. I was back to being a normal guy, and could now focus on enjoying my family life. My mind would no longer need to work continuously on trying to solve life-or-death puzzles. I was free.

Part V

Epilogue

An agent once told me that being in the FBI was something like finding out about the true nature of our reality, a theme depicted in science fiction, including the movie *The Matrix*. Most people in life just take the "blue pill." They live in their own little universe, blind to many of the forces that drive the world, both good and bad. But when an agent joins the FBI, he or she is swallowing a "red pill." He or she learns about things that he or she could have never imagined. Many of those things are bad. Our eyes are pried open. Things are never quite the same once a person looks under the hood of the world with the perspective of an FBI agent. But to some degree, time has eroded my undesirable memories about the worst parts of our society, and I have returned to having a generally positive outlook about people and the world we live in.

I now work for the State of Texas and perform long-term strategic planning for IT systems and operations. My IT job certainly does not have the excitement or prestige in the public's eye that my former FBI job had. When introducing myself to someone, the phrase "I'm a TOGAF certified Enterprise Architect" somehow does not have the same effect as "I'm an FBI agent." I love my job, but when describing my work I tend to elicit yawns from the recipients of my conversation. However, I know that my contributions to society with my current job exceed what I did as an FBI agent. My skillset is much better used. I am a much happier person. I enjoy every day; I enjoy life. And I make a difference for the citizens of the state, even if I do not see the results directly like I did in the FBI.

I have never forgotten the words of the FBI Defensive Tactics instructor who had allowed me to pass the pushups portion of my fitness test, but pulled me aside and told me to never settle for anything less than my best effort. With an inner drive to continue to challenge myself, and with encouragement from my niece in Chicago, I decided to register for the Chicago marathon. On September 1, 2010, in preparation for the race, I was enjoying a long training run around Ladybird Lake in Austin, Texas. I rounded a corner on the trail by the water and came across a gathering of nearly twenty people staring at the lake. Aside from the sound of traffic on the nearby Lamar Bridge, there was silence. Silence, that is, until I heard a woman's screams coming from the lake, which were then cut off because her head disappeared underwater.

She was drowning. Nobody was helping. I immediately ripped my music player and headphones off, jumped in the lake, and swam about thirty yards out to the woman in distress. I reached her while she was still near the surface, and despite her desperately flailing arms, I managed to lift her head out of the water enough that she could get some air. In the meantime, two other men swam out to help. The three of us were able to successfully pull the thrashing woman back to shore and out of the water to the safety of dry land, where she coughed up some water but was otherwise physically ok. On that day I contributed to saving the life of a person, and I didn't even need a badge or gun to do so.

The world turns because of all types of people in different professions. The FBI is really not adding "value" to the economy, at least not in the same way that workers add to the Gross Domestic Product when building cars, designing football stadiums, or programming smartphone applications. Agents stamp out problems caused by criminals, but if one looks ahead optimistically towards the United States having a good workforce and a more productive society, many years down the road, need for FBI agents could cease to exist. An unarmed man or woman sitting in a corporate cube can make more of a difference than a machine gun-toting FBI agent to society. The FBI has heroes, but so do the cube-filled corporate and government halls throughout America. Doctors, nurses, marketing managers, sanitation truck drivers, real estate agents, salespeople, and McDonald's employees all help drive the economy and make our country the best in the world. Sometimes people only need to understand that their impact may not be directly seen. We are all small cogs in a big machine, but those cogs are critical to the nation, our economy, and our way of life.

If asked what my advice would be to someone who is interested in becoming an agent, I would reply, "Be bold and fearless, and if your dream is to be an FBI agent, by all means give it a shot." But when people apply to be in the FBI and they do not make it in, they should know that life may have even bigger, better, and more important roles in store for them. We all should try to make the most of every single day, and remember that as John Lennon sang, "Life is what happens to you while you're busy making other plans."

THE END

Purchase other Black Rose Writing titles at www.blackrosewriting.com/books
and use promo code PRINT to receive a 20% discount.

BLACK ROSE
writing™

CPSIA information can be obtained at www.ICGtesting.com
Printed in the USA
LVOW10s1733220316

480284LV00012B/221/P